T0353875

40 YEARS OF TRIAL & ERROR

Mom's Favorite Recipes & Memoirs

Darlene Dunkin

iUniverse, Inc.
New York   Bloomington

40 YEARS OF TRIAL & ERROR
Mom's Favorite Recipes & Memoirs

Copyright © 2009 Darlene Dunkin

All rights reserved. No part of this book may be used or reproduced by any means, graphic, electronic, or mechanical, including photocopying, recording, taping or by any information storage retrieval system without the written permission of the publisher except in the case of brief quotations embodied in critical articles and reviews.

iUniverse books may be ordered through booksellers or by contacting:

iUniverse
1663 Liberty Drive
Bloomington, IN 47403
www.iuniverse.com
1-800-Authors (1-800-288-4677)

Because of the dynamic nature of the Internet, any Web addresses or links contained in this book may have changed since publication and may no longer be valid. The views expressed in this work are solely those of the author and do not necessarily reflect the views of the publisher, and the publisher hereby disclaims any responsibility for them.

ISBN: 978-1-4401-2794-6 (pbk)
ISBN: 978-1-4401-2795-3 (ebk)

Printed in the United States of America

iUniverse rev. date: 5/22/09

INTRODUCTION

I would like to start by telling you a little about my life growing up. My father was a bartender and my mom stayed home caring for him and us children. We were a poor family. My father was an alcoholic, abusive and controlling. Mom did the best she could with what was provided to her. She was an honest, kind woman who loved her children and did not really know that there were other choices in her life until a later time. I had two older brothers, Richard and Edward, Richard being the oldest. Richard was my best friend and confidant. He was an overweight child and our father used to beat him for it. I will never know how he survived all the abuse he received just for being overweight, but it never broke his spirit. At the age of eighteen he suffered a severe heart attach. He overcame, lost some weight and continued on to medical school. He was my inspiration to continue on. My brother was so talented in many ways, smart, fun to be around, an incredibly artist and had a voice of an opera singer. He was killed in a car accident at the age of 21. Losing him in my life was extremely devastating. At this time I was a single mom with a soon to be one year old son. Having been emancipated from my parents, outside of my brother Richard, I had no family or friends to fall back on for any type of support. My brother Edward and I never really saw eye to eye and he never wanted to have much to do with me. My parents divorced when I was around ten years of age. My father refused to pay support and left my mom to find outside work with no education or previous employment experience. She worked the rest of her days with minimum paying jobs. My mother was of a kind and beautiful spirit. Myself, a mother of two sons and on my own, I was determined to give my boys the best I could. At that time this meant a clean, warm place to live and food to survive. Asked to leave school, even though I was a good student, raged me and gave me even more determination to show that I could be a good mother and provider. Only finishing the eight grade, I continued on my own to receive my GED and went to a few community college business classes. It was all I could do to pay the rent and feed my sons. Working one, two and sometimes three jobs, I always tried to make sure that we were together for dinner time. It was our time to eat, visit, and talk. This was our special time together, sometimes laughing and sometimes crying. When my boys reached of school age I was fortunate to meet someone who later I married and adopted my sons as his own. Cooking through the years was a joy for me. I have been fortunate to have traveled to many places in the states and also overseas. In my travels I have tasted many food variations and recipes. Returning home, there were many times I incorporated these new foods into our diet. Except for rare occasions our busy schedules never kept us from gathering at the kitchen table for dinner. These were times to discuss our daily events and tomorrows schedule. It was a good time to hear about school, new friends and differences in opinions. After my sons grew into adults and ventured out on their own, I went through an unexpected divorce. I have since remarried and my husband and I reside on 16 acres of wooded property surrounded by farm land. We raise our own beef and pork and have chickens for their eggs. When we get fish hungry, we fish out of our small catfish pond. I raise a large garden every year that I share with my family and friends. I also do a large amount of canning which we enjoy all year long. I continue to be a part of my son's families, watching their careers and the new grand children come in to play. Surviving three car accidents I am thankful for every day I wake. I have been blessed with two wonderful daughter-in-laws and seven beautiful grandchildren. Both my sons do the majority of cooking in their household. This works for them and I am proud that my sons do well in the kitchen. I hate the old saying that the kitchen is a woman's place. This is so wrong and misunderstood. I listen to people say that they don't like to cook because of the kitchen cleanup. This has a lot to do with the kitchen being unorganized. With a little time and effort the kitchen can be a friendly and fun place to be. Involve the whole family to assist with the chopping, cooking and clean up. While you are all together in the kitchen you may find yourselves involved in some fun and interesting conversations. Cooking has been a large part of my life and has brought much joy and rewarding experiences with both my family and friends. I have been cooking since the age of nine, trying and testing recipes from hundreds of cookbooks. For the past five years my oldest son has wanted me to get all my recipes into a book form. His aspiration and support allowed me to follow through with his wishes. As you will see in this book there are no serving amounts or nutritional values listed. I believe this is just common sense. Most of my recipes, unless noted, will serve an average family of four. I consider myself a reasonably healthy cook. I do very little deep frying and include a lot of vegetables in our diet. There are many choices of low fat & no cholesterol ingredients, salad dressings, margarines and shredded cheeses available. This is a matter of taste and choice. Use the ingredients that best suit you and your diet. I believe you can eat almost anything in moderation. Cooking can be fun and a really wonderful way to bring family and friends together, especially in today's busy society. We all have to eat, sooner or later. I have compiled recipes for all these years, adding and subtracting ingredients, making them into tasty nutritional dishes. Don't stop making a recipe that looks interesting because it may have an ingredient you don't like. Eliminate the ingredient you don't like, add something in its place or just switch it around a little to you and your family's liking. My oldest son likes it spicy but his wife doesn't, so he compromises. My youngest son and his wife like it bland, so they leave out all the spicy extras. You will see that in a lot of my recipes there are three ingredients I use frequently, being onions, peppers and garlic. If this is not your cup of tea, leave them out or substitute for something that is. Nothing is written in stone. I truly hope you will enjoy this cookbook. After 40 years of trial and error I still refer to all these recipes as a reference in my own kitchen. I would be lost without them. Start in the kitchen, making some lasting memories. Material things are nice to have but memories are the only thing you will pass on forever.

Table of Contents

MOM'S
FAVORITE RECIPES
&
MEMOIRS

40 YEARS
OF
TRIAL & ERROR

*TASTY, SIMPLE, EASY TO FOLLOW RECIPES

*IN A PINCH SUBSTITUTIONS

*HELPFUL HINTS

*YEARS OF TESTING, EXPERIMENTATION &
CREATIVE COOKING

*MEMORABLE FOOD STORIES

*NOT YOUR EVERYDAY COOKBOOK

IN A PINCH
SUBSTITUTIONS
&
HELPFUL HINTS

- **INGREDIENT EQUIVALENTS**
- **COOKING TERMS**
- **FOOD STORAGE**
- **ORGANIZING THE KITCHEN**
- **LEFTOVERS**
- **WEIGHTS & MEASURES**

INGREDIENT:	SUBSTITUTIONS:
Allspice : 1 tsp.	½ tsp. cinnamon plus 1/8 tsp. ground cloves
Baking Powder:1 tsp.	¼ tsp. baking soda plus 5/8 tsp. cream of tarter
Bread Crumbs, Dry: ¼ cup	1 slice bread toasted and cubed
Butter:1 cup	1 cup margarine or solid shortening or 7/8 cup lard
Buttermilk: 1 cup	1 cup plain yogurt
Chocolate, Unsweetened: 1 oz.	3 tbs. cocoa plus 1 tbs. butter
Corn Starch: 1 Tbs.	2 tbs. flour
Corn Syrup, Light: 1 cup	1 cup maple syrup
Corn Syrup, Dark: 1 cup	¾ cup light corn syrup plus ¼ cup molasses
Cracker Crumbs: ¾ cup	1 cup bread crumbs
Cream, Heavy: 1 cup	¾ cup milk plus 1/3 cup melted butter (will not whip)
Cream, Light: 1 cup	7/8 cup milk plus 3 tbs. melted butter
Cream, Whipping: 1 cup	2/3 cup chilled evaporated milk , whipped
Egg: 1 whole	2 yolks
Flour, All Purpose: 1 cup	1-1/8 cup cake flour or 1 cup cornmeal
Flour, Cake: 1 cup	1 cup minus 2 tbs. all purpose flour
Flour, Self-Rising: 1 cup	1 cup all-purpose, 1-1/4 tsp baking powder, ¼ tsp salt
Garlic: 1 sm. clove	1/8 tsp. garlic powder or ½ tsp instant minced
Herbs, Dried: 1 tsp	1 Tbs. fresh & minced
Honey: 1 cup	1-1/4 cup sugar plus 1/2 cup liquid
Lemon Juice: 1 tsp.	½ tsp. vinegar
Lemon, Rind Grated: 1 tsp.	½ tsp lemon extract
Milk, Skim: 1 cup	½ cup instant powdered milk plus ¾ cup water
Milk, Whole: 1 cup	½ cup evaporated milk plus ½ cup water
Milk, to Sour: 1 cup	1 cup (less 1 Tbs.) milk plus 1 Tbs. vinegar or lemon
Molasses: 1 cup	1 cup honey
Mustard, Prepared: 1 Tbs.	1 tsp. dry mustard
Onion Chopped: 1 sm.	1 Tbs. instant minced or 1 tsp. onion powder
Sour Cream: 1 cup	7/8 cup buttermilk or plain yogurt, 3 Tbs. melted butter
Sugar, granulated: 1 cup	1-3/4 confectioner's sugar (Do not substitute in baking) or 2 cups corn syrup
Sugar, Confection: 1 cup	½ cup plus 1 Tbs. granulated sugar
Sugar, Brown: 1 cup	1 cup sugar plus 1 Tbs. honey
Tomatoes, Canned: 1 cup	½ cup tomato sauce plus ½ cup water plus 1-1/3 cup chopped tomatoes
Tomato, Juice: 1 cup	½ cup tomato sauce plus ½ cup water, dash of salt & Sugar or paste &3/4 cup water, dash of salt & sugar
Tomato, Ketchup: ½ cup	½ cup tomato sauce plus 2 tbs. sugar, 1 tbs. vinegar, And 1/8 tsp. ground cloves
Tomato, Puree: 1 cup	½ cup tomato paste plus ½ cup water
Tomato, Sauce: 1 cup	1 can (3 oz.) tomato paste plus ½ cup water
Tomato, Soup: 1 can	1 cup tomato sauce plus ¼ cup water
Vanilla Extract:	Imitation vanilla
Yogurt, Plain: 1 cup	1 cup buttermilk

INGREDIENT EQUIVALENTS

INGREDIENT	EQUIVALENT
Chocolate: 1 cup pieces	6 ounce pkg. chips
1 ounce unsweetened	1 square unsweetened
Crumbs: 1 cup bread cubes	2 slices bread
1 cup bread crumbs (soft)	1-1/2 to 2 slices bread
1 cup bread crumbs (dry)	4 slices bread
Graham Cracker Crumbs: 1 cup	14 graham cracker squares
Vanilla Wafer Crumbs: 1 cup (fine)	22 vanilla wafers
Chocolate Wafer Crumbs: 1 cup	19 wafers
Gingersnap Crumbs: 1 cup (fine)	15 gingersnaps
Butter or margarine: ½ cup	1 stick (1/4 pound)
Cream Cheese: 1 cup	8 ounce pkg.
Blue Cheese: 1 cup (crumbled)	4 ounces blue cheese
Cheese Grated: 1-1/4 cups	¼ pound hard cheese (Romano & Parmesan)
Hard Cheese Shredded: 1 cup	4 ounces hard cheese (Cheddar & Swiss)
Soft Cheese Shredded: 1-1/4 cup	4 ounces soft cheese (American & Monterey Jack)
Whipped Cream: 2 cups	1 cup heavy cream or 1 cup whipping cream
Almonds Chopped: 3 to 3-1/2 cups	1 pound, shelled
Pecans Chopped: 4 cups	1 pound shelled
Walnuts Chopped: 4 cups	1 pound, shelled
Pasta Cooked: 2 to 2-1/2 cups (pasta varies / depending on size)	¼ pound, uncooked
Rice Cooked: 3 cups	1 cup raw
Granulated Sugar: 2 cups	1 pound
Brown Sugar: 2-1/4 cups (packed firm)	1 pound
Confectioner's Sugar: 3-1/3 to 4 cups	1 pound
Miscellaneous:	
Bacon Crumbled: ½ cup	8 slices bacon
Beans/Pease (dried): 1 cup	½ pound dried
Beans/Peas (cooked): 2-1/4 to 2-1/2 cups	1 cup dried
Broth: 1 cup	1 bouillon cube plus 1 cup water
Chicken (cooked): 2 cups	1 lg. boned whole chicken breast
Chicken (cooked): 3 cups	3-1/2 pound whole chicken
Herbs (fresh): 1 tablespoon	1 teaspoon dried

VEGETABLE EQUIVALENTS

Asparagus: 1 pound = 3 cups chopped
Beans (string): 1 pound = 4 cups chopped
Beets: 1 pound (5 medium) = 2-1/2 cups chopped
Broccoli: ½ pound = 6 cups chopped
Cabbage: 1 pound = 4-1/2 cups shredded
Carrots: 1 pound = 3-1/2 cups sliced or grated
Celery: 1 pound = 4 cups chopped
Cucumbers: 1 pound (2 medium) = 4 cups sliced
Eggplant: 1 pound = 4 cups chopped
Garlic: 1 clove = 1 teaspoon chopped
Leeks: 1 pound = 4 cups chopped (2 cups cooked)
Mushrooms: 1 pound = 5-6 cups sliced (2 cups cooked)
Onions: 1 pound = 4 cups sliced (2 cups cooked)
Peas: 1 pound whole = 1 to 1-1/2 cups shelled
Potatoes: 1 pound (3 medium) = 2 cups mashed
Pumpkin 1 pound = 4 cups chopped (2 cups cooked)
Spinach: 1 pound = ¾ to 1 cup cooked
Squash (summer): 1 pound = 4 cups grated
Squash (winter): 2 pounds = 2-1/2 cups cooked, pureed
Sweet Potatoes: 1 pound = 4 cups grated (1 cup cooked, pureed
Swiss Chard: 1 pound = 5 to 6 packed leaves = 1 to 1-1/2 cups cooked
Tomatoes: 1 pound (3-4 medium) = 1-1/2 cups seeded pulp
Turnips: 1 pound = 4 cups chopped = 2 cups mashed

FRUIT EQUIVALENTS

Apples: 1 pound (3-4 medium) = 3 cups sliced
Bananas: 1 pound (3-4 medium) = 1-3/4 cups mashed
Berries: 1 quart = 3-1/2 cups
Dates: 1 pound = 2-1/2 cups pitted
Lemon: 1 whole = 1 to 3 tablespoon juice & 1 to 1-1/2 teaspoons grated rind
Lime: 1 whole: = 1-1/2 to 2 tablespoon juice
Orange: 1 medium = 6 to 8 tablespoon juice & 2 to 3 tablespoon grated rind
Peaches: 1 pound (4 medium) = 3 cups sliced
Pears: 1 pound (4 medium) = 2 cups sliced
Rhubarb: 1 pound = 2 cups cooked
Strawberries: 1 quart = 4 cups sliced

COOKING TERMS:

Au Jus: Natural juices from cooked meat.

Blanch: To cook for a short time in boiling water. Bring to a boil, place ingredients for a few minutes (stop boiling). Remove and rinse with cold water. This method is used a lot when canning or freezing fresh vegetables.

Degrease: To remove fat from surface of a cooking liquid by chilling so that the fat congeals on top and is easily lifted off.

Dredge: To coat food lightly by dipping in flour and shaking off the excess.

Flambe' : To ignite alcoholic ingredients such as brandy to burn off alcoholic taste.

Fold: To combine ingredients with a gentle motion usually with a lg. spatula, scooping the mixture from the bottom and turning itself over.

Julienne: To cut vegetables or cheeses in thin strips resembling matchsticks.

Marinate: To combine foods with ingredients that tenderize and add flavor before cooking or serving.

Mince: To cut or chop into very fine pieces.

Puree: To mash or blend until smooth.

Roux: A cooked mixture of flour and fat used to thicken sauces.

Scald: To heat a liquid just until the boiling point. Milk is scalded when a ring of small bubbles forms around the edge of the cooking pan.

Sear: To brown the exterior of a food, hot and fast, usually for meat, which is then cooked completely at a lower temperature. The best way to BBQ a steak is to sear it.

Shred: To cut food in short, thin strips with a grater or food processor.

Simmer: To cook just below a boil.

Skim: To scrape fat or foam from the surface of a cooking liquid. This is often used in canning jams and jelly.

Stock: Flavorful liquid made by simmering meat bones, meats, vegetables, & spices, in water.

Zest: Colored part of the rind of a citrus fruit. Use a grater. Only use colored part.

FOOD STORAGE

Get the most out of your ingredients by storing them properly.

Baking Powder: Store in a cool and dry place. Store airtight (after opened I store in a zip lock bag). 6 months

Baking Soda: Store the same as Baking Powder

Dry Beans: Once the pkg. is open, do not store in the refrigerator. Store in air tight container or zip lock in a cool, dry, dark place. 1 year

Brown Sugar: Store sugar wrapped tight . 4 months

Chocolate: Store in a cool place 60-75 F. 1 year. (I store excess of chocolate in the freezer)

Dried Fruit: Store unopened pkg. in cool, dry place or refrigerator. Store opened pkgs. Airtight in refrigerator or freezer. 6-8 months

Flour: Store in a clean, tightly covered container at room temperature. 1 year

Garlic: Store whole garlic in airy, dark and cool place. Store opened minced garlic in refrigerator, sealed.

Granulated sugar: Store sugar in a clean, tightly covered container. 2 years

Nuts: Store in a zip lock, rolled tight, in refrigerator or freezer.

Potatoes: Store in a dark, cool place. I have good luck storing them in the bottom shelf of the refrigerator.

Prepared Foods & Leftovers: Cool hot foods to room temperature. Always store covered in the refrigerator.

Shredded coconut: Store airtight in a cool place. Do not store in refrigerator.

Fresh vegetables: I store vegi's loosely in the bottom food drawers in the refrigerator. After cutting in to a vegetable such as lettuce or a cucumber, wrap tight in saran wrap.

Yeast: Store opened yeast air tight. Store in refrigerator or freezer.

MY FAVORITE FOOD ITEMS TO KEEP IN STOCK

Cooking Spray: I use this to grease all my pots and pans.
Cooking Oil
Pepper
Season Salt: I like creole
Garlic Powder
Celery Salt
Onion Powder
Parsley Flakes
Beef & Chicken Bouillon:
Vanilla
Baking Soda
Baking Powder
Cornstarch
Flour
Sugar
Bread
Crackers
Milk: (or evaporated milk)
Sour Cream
Shredded Cheese: I store my extra cheese in the freezer

Pantry:
Mustard
Mayonnaise or salad dressing: I use mostly salad dressing in my recipes.
Cream of mushroom, celery & chicken soup
Tomato soup, sauce, paste & stewed tomatoes

Fresh Vegetables:
Onions
Bell Peppers
Potatoes
Minced Garlic: I like the minced garlic you buy a jar. Keep it refrigerated after opening.

Other Items:
Meat Injector
Quart Jar with Lid: I use this a lot for mixing and shaking.
Mixer, blender or food processor
Wood mixing spoons
Measuring Cup: (See thru with different measurements)
Teflon Spatula: Never use metal utensils to stir in a Teflon Pan
Thin Latex Disposable Gloves: Use these when handling and cleaning hot peppers.
Pots & Pans: I have my favorite frying pan, my favorite saucepan and my favorite casserole dish.

ORGANIZING THE KITCHEN

Keep an area clear near the stove and/or sink for chopping and mixing.

Keep seasonings near the stove or work area. (At least most common used)

Keep your most often used pots, pans, casserole dishes and mixing bowls, in a reachable area for easy access.

Keep flour and sugar in canisters with tight fitting lids and also easily accessible.

Keep refrigerator clean of spoiling foods.

Keep an empty (metal) coffee can, soup can, etc. for used grease storage. Do not pour grease down the sink. Place in empty can, cool until it hardens & dispose.

Keep your food pantry organized & rotated. Know where to locate your food items that you will need for a recipe.

Keep your dishes washed as you work. If you do not have a dishwasher it is so much easier than having them pile up and harden.

Keep your garbage can close to your work area. (Good cooks have a lot of garbage) My son keeps his garbage can in a cabinet. When I am at his house cooking in the kitchen, the garbage can comes out until I finish.

Keep your kitchen clean and organized. It really makes a difference.

LEFTOVERS

Put Your Leftovers To Good Use. Don't Let Them Go To Waste.

*To much leftover turkey or chicken? Cook up a soup, casserole or stir fry dish.

*Leftover hamburgers or meat loaf? Add it to a rice & vegetable dish.

*Vegetables piling up in the refrigerator? Make a salad, soup, stew or stir fry.

*Fruit getting ripe? Make a fruit crisp or some fruity muffins.

*Need to use up some sour cream or cream cheese? Whip up a stroganoff dish.

*Cooked to big of a Roast? Make some French Dips, soup or stir fry dish.

*Is milk about to expire? Make some gravy. (Good time for biscuits & gravy)

*The Bread getting stale? Stuffing is always a good side dish.

*Leftover hamburger or hot dog buns? Turn them into garlic bread.

*Make to many mashed potatoes? Have some potato patties with your breakfast.

*Flour tortillas leftover? Make some breakfast burritos, quesadillas or fajitas.

FREEZE YOUR LEFTOVERS

You can freeze almost all your leftovers to use or eat at a later date. Here are some suggestions for freezing.

*Whatever you are freezing, seal it as airtight as possible, so it won't freezer burn.

*Make up small meals (like TV dinners) to heat up on those busy/tired days.

*If you make waffles for breakfast, make some extra to freeze for those running late mornings. Take them out of the freezer and pop them in the toaster.

*Blanch your raw vegetables before freezing and use them later for soups, stews or stir fry.

*Turn your ripe fruit into freezer jam.

*Freeze your extra cheese's (block or shredded) for later use that calls for shredded cheese.

FOOD WEIGHTS & MEASURES

WEIGHT/MEASURE	EQUIVALENT
Dash	less than a teaspoon
1-1/2 teaspoons	½ tablespoon
3 teaspoons	1 tablespoon
1 tablespoon	½ fluid ounce
2 tablespoons	1/8 cup (1 fluid ounce)
4 tablespoons	¼ cup (2 fluid ounces)
5-1/3 tablespoons	1/3 cup
8 tablespoons	½ cup (4 fluid ounces)
10-2/3 tablespoon	2/3 cup
12 tablespoons	¾ cup (6 fluid ounces)
16 tablespoons	1 cup (6 fluid ounces)
3/8 cup	¼ cup plus 2 tablespoons
5/8 cup	½ cup plus 2 tablespoons
7/8 cup	¾ cup plus 2 tablespoons
1 cup	½ pint (8 fluid ounces)
2 cups	1 pint (16 fluid ounces)
4 cups	1 quart (32 fluid ounces)
2 pints	1 quart
2 quarts	½ gallon
4 quarts (liquid)	1 gallon
8 quarts (dry)	1 peck
4 pecks	1 bushel
16 ounces (dry)	1 pound
1 gram	.035 ounces
1 kilogram	2.21 pounds
1 ounce	28.35 grams
1 liter	1.06 quarts or 1,000 milliliters

BREAKFAST

A lesson to learn is that you are never to old, experienced or good enough to learn something new. After 40 years of cooking I was dumbfounded after an experience with my youngest son, Alan. He was home visiting and one morning he decided to cook his own breakfast. Delighted that he was cooking, I was eager to watch. Making an omelet, he beat his eggs in a bowl and poured them into a pan. I pondered if he knew when it was the perfect time to add the cheese and other ingredients on top. To my surprise, he flipped the eggs after browning for a few seconds, placed everything in, flopped it in half and BAM, cooked the perfect omelet. All these years I wondered why I had runny omelets. His simple solution of flipping the eggs before adding the ingredients eliminated this problem. Now, in the mornings, my husband and I enjoy the ultimate omelet. (Omelet)

BREAKFAST COBBLER

1/3 cup firmly packed brown sugar
2 tbs. quick cooking tapioca
1 tsp. cinnamon
1 tbs. lemon juice
¼ cup water
4 apples, peeled and sliced
1/3 cups raisins

Oat Crunch:

1/3 cup butter or margarine
1/3 cup rolled oats
3 tbs. sugar
¾ cup flour
Mix together until crumbly

Preheat oven to 375. Mix all ingredients together except oat crunch. Place in greased 2 qt. casserole dish. Bake at 375 for 15 minutes. Remove from oven and stir fruit mixture. Crumble oat crunch over top. Bake 35-40 minutes or until browned. Serve warm.

SAUSAGE ROLLS

2 cups bisquick
1 cup water
1 cup shredded cheddar cheese
½ lb. Hot sausage
½ lb. Regular sausage
Note: or use 1 lb. or your choice of sausage

Mix all together. Drop heaping teaspoon on a greased cookie sheet. Bake at 400 for 20 minutes.

BREAKFAST BURRITOS

6 lg. flour tortillas
10 eggs
1 lb. sausage
½ cup chopped onion
½ cup fine chopped bell pepper
Salt & pepper to taste
Salsa – mild, medium or hot
6 tbs. sour cream

Lay out 6 lg. tortillas. Place 1 tbs. of sour cream on each tortilla. Spread. Brown sausage, onion, pepper, salt and pepper. Set aside. Scramble eggs. Divide sausage mixture and eggs evenly on tortillas. Top with 2 tbs. salsa. Fold up each side and roll up. Microwave each 1 minute.

OMELET

2-3 eggs
¼ cup cheese (your choice)
¼ cup diced meat (cooked ham, bacon or sausage)
Note: use all three meats for the Ultimate meat lovers omelet
Extras are optional: onion, bell pepper, mushrooms ,salsa
Note; Extras are better if you sauté them in a little butter or margarine

Whisk or blend eggs until fluffy. Pour in heated sm. omelet pan. Cook over medium heat until bottom is slightly brown. Flip. Add cheese, meat and extras.
Fold over in half. Flip once more until both sides are golden brown.

MAKE-AHEAD BRUNCH

8 frozen hash brown patties
1 pkg. (8 oz.) thinly sliced ham, chopped
1-1/4 cups shredded cheddar cheese
2 cups milk
1 can cream of mushroom soup
6 eggs
1 tsp. ground mustard
¼ tsp. pepper

Place hash brown patties in a greased 13 X 9 X 2 baking pan. Top with ham and 1 cup of cheese. Combine milk, soup, eggs, mustard, and pepper. Pour over cheese. Cover and refrigerate overnight. Remove from frig ,30 minutes before baking. Bake at 350 for 1 hour. Uncover and sprinkle with remaining cheese. Bake additional 20-25 minutes, or until center is tested by inserting a knife. If knife comes out clean, it is ready. Let stand 10 minutes before serving.

BREAKFAST CASSEROLE

8 hard boiled eggs
2 cups grated swiss cheese or thin sliced swiss
1 can cream of mushroom soup
¾ cup milk
½ tsp. salt
¼ tsp. pepper
1 tbs. prepared mustard
1 tbs. chopped onion or onion flakes
1 tbs. butter
1 lb. cubed ham
Rye bread

Grease a 13 X 9 X 2 baking pan. Slice and layer eggs evenly in pan. Spread swiss cheese over eggs. Set aside. Mix soup, milk, salt, pepper, mustard, and onion. Pour over cheese. Place ham over mixture. Butter rye bread. Place bread over ham. Bake at 350 for 40 minutes.

Note: If making the night before. Don't add ham and bread until just before baking.

BLT EGG BAKE

¼ cup mayonnaise
5 slices of bread, toasted
4 slices American cheese
12 strips of bacon, cooked and crumbled
4 eggs
1 med. tomato, halved and sliced
2 tbs. butter or margarine
2 tbs. flour
¼ tsp. salt
1/8 tsp. pepper
1 cup milk
1.2 cup shredded cheddar cheese
2 green onions, chopped

Spread mayo on one side of toasted bread. Cut into sm. pieces. Place in a greased 8 X 8 cooking pan. Top with cheese slices and bacon. Set aside. Fry eggs until yolk is cooked. Place eggs over bacon. Top with tomato slices. Set aside. In a saucepan, melt butter. Stir in flour, salt and pepper. Stir until smooth. Add milk gradually. Bring to boil, stirring constantly. Cook until thickened. Pour over tomato. Sprinkle shredded cheese and onion over hot mixture. Bake, uncovered at 325 for 10 minutes.

OMELETTE BRUNCH

10 eggs
3-1/2 cup milk
6 slices white buttered bread, cubed
1 pkg. smoked sausages
1 lb. bacon, cooked and crumbled
2 cups shredded cheddar cheese
½ onion chopped (optional)
1 bell pepper chopped (optional)
1 can mushrooms, drained (optional)

Place bread cubes in a greased 13 X 9 baking pan. Spread the shredded cheese over the bread. If using onion, pepper and mushrooms, sauté with bacon. Place bacon and sausage over cheese. Beat eggs and milk. Pour over meat. Bake at 350 for 1 hour.

Note: This dish can be made ahead and refrigerated overnight.

SOUPS

My son's, Carl and Alan, will never let me forget about the day I made Split Pea Soup. Young teenagers at the time, I had been on a rampage with them about getting their dirty laundry in the hamper. Everyday I was hearing "Where is my baseball uniform or where is my football uniform", etc, etc. I finally gave up and told them they could start doing their own laundry. They didn't take me serious until they ran out of clean clothes. In the meantime, I decided to make a big pot of split pea soup. It seemed to have taken me the entire day and there was enough to feed an army. Dinner time came and soup was on. This was a dish that none of us had ever tasted. Normally there was always conversation going on, but this night it was extremely quiet around the kitchen table. Knowing that I had been upset with them and walking on egg shells in my presence, I did not say anything. After taking a taste of my soup, to my surprise, it was Horrible. When I asked them why no one would tell me how awful it was they told me they thought if they complained they would have to start doing their own cooking. It has become a big family joke and my sons will still not eat split pea soup. Don't worry, my recipe has been perfected since then. (Split Pea Soup)

POTATO SOUP

6 potatoes, peeled and cubed (bite size)
1 lg. onion, chopped
2 carrots, peeled and sliced thin (or chop in food processor)
3 stalks celery, chopped
4 chicken bouillon cubes or equivalent
1 tbs. parsley flakes
4 cups water
1 tsp. salt
½ tsp. celery salt
1/8 tsp. garlic powder (optional)
½ tsp. pepper
1 (13 oz.) can evaporated milk

Put all ingredients in a crock pot except milk. Cover and cook on high for 3-4 hours. Turn to low for additional 6-7 hours. Stir in milk during last hour.

Helpful Hints: If wanting a thicker soup. Add 3 tbs. flour to milk in a jar. Shake Well. Pour into soup mixture. Stir Quickly.

HAM/POTATO SOUP

Use potato soup recipe. Add 1-1/2 cubes cubed ham

CHEESY POTATO SOUP

Use potato soup recipe. Add 1-1/2 cup of shredded American cheese or processed cheese.

CLAM CHOWDER

Use potato soup recipe. Instead of cubing potatoes, Dice them into smaller pcs. Add. 1 cup cooked clams or canned clams, drained.

TOMATO SOUP

38 oz. of canned chopped tomatoes canned or fresh, peeled and seeded
10 oz. green chili peppers, chopped or fresh , chopped
14 oz. can chicken broth or bouillon (Make equivalent to)
½ cup chopped celery
½ cup chopped onion
1 tbs. parsley or cilantro
1 tbs. sugar
1 tbs. lime juice

In a lg. saucepan, cook all ingredients down. Simmer for 20 minutes. Stirring as needed. Cool. Blend soup mixture in a processor or blender until smooth. Reheat to serve.

CREAM OF ASPARGUS SOUP

1 pkg. (10 oz.) frozen asparagus, thawed or equivalent fresh cooked down
¼ cup chopped onion
1 can (14oz.) chicken broth, divided
2 tbs. butter or margarine
2 tbs. flour
½ tsp celery salt
1-1/2 cups milk
½ cup sour cream
2 tsp. lemon juice
½ tsp grated lemon peel (optional)

In a lg. saucepan, cook asparagus, onion and ½ broth for 5 minutes. Cool. Blend in blender or processor until smooth. In same saucepan add other 1/2 broth, butter, flour and celery salt. Cook and stir until thick. Add asparagus mixture and milk. Heat. Gradually add sour cream and lemon. Heat but do not boil.

BEAN SOUP

1 lb. dry beans of your choice (soak overnight, drain)
2 quarts water
1 lb. smoked pork meat pcs., ham chunks, or ham bones
1 tsp. celery salt
1 tsp. creole or season salt
½ tsp. pepper
1 tsp. onion powder

Put all ingredients in crock pot. Cover and cook on high for 5 hours. Turn to low and cook additional 5 hours or until done.

SPLIT PEA SOUP

Use bean soup recipe. Substitute beans for dry split peas. Follow same directions. Use 1 quart water instead of 2.

CREAMY CORN CHOWDER

2 chicken bouillon
1 cup water
5 bacon strips
1 cup chopped bell pepper
½ cup chopped onion
¼ cup flour
3 cups milk
1-1/2 cup kernel corn
1 can cream style corn
1-1/2 tsp. creole or season salt
1/8 tsp. pepper
1/8 tsp. dried basil

Dissolve bouillon in water. Set aside. Cook bacon until crisp. Save drippings. Drain & crumble. Saute bell pepper and onion in drippings until tender. Add flour and cook till bubbly. Gradually stir in milk and bouillon. Bring to boil stirring constantly. Cook until thickened. In a lg saucepan add cooking mixture with corn, bacon, and seasoning. Cook for 10 minutes or heated through.

HAM & CORN CHOWDER

Use corn chowder receipe. Add 1 cup chopped ham.

BROCOLLI CHOWDER

10 oz. frozen broccoli, thawed
2 tbs. minced onion
½ cup water
½ tsp. salt
2 cups milk
1 can cream of mushroom soup
1 cup chunked processed cheese
1 lg. potatoes, diced and cooked

Put all ingredients in saucepan. Mix. Cook until hot.

CHEESEBURGER SOUP

½ lb. ground beef, browned and drained
¾ cup onion
¾ cup shredded carrots
¾ cups diced celery
1 tsp. parsley
1 tsp. basil (optional)
4 tbs. butter or margarine, divided
3 cups chicken broth
4 cups peeled and diced potatoes
¼ cup flour
2 cups cubed or shredded American cheese
1-1/2 cups milk
¾ tsp. salt
½ tsp. pepper
¼ cup sour cream

Mix flour into drained cooked beef. Put all other ingredients (except sour cream) in crock pot. Mix. Cook high for 2-3 hours. Turn to low for additional 4-5 hours or until potatoes are tender. Add sour cream last few minutes of cooking

Note: Speed it up by pre-cooking potatoes and carrots. Place all ingredients (except sour cream) in a lg. saucepan. Heat to boiling, stirring often. Simmer for additional 10 minutes. Add sour cream last few minutes of cooking.

CHICKEN VEGETABLE SOUP

4 cups chicken broth
1 lb. boiled boneless chunked chicken pcs. or boil down a whole chicken
Cool; and take chicken meat off the bone
½ cup flour
1 onion, chopped
1 cup shredded carrots
1-1/2 cups chopped celery
1 chopped bell pepper (optional)
1 cup chopped yellow squash (optional)
1 cup peeled, diced eggplant (optional)
1 tsp. celery salt
1 tsp. pepper
1 tsp. creole or season salt
½ tsp garlic powder
1 dash hot sauce (optional)

Coat cooked chicken with flour. Put in crock pot. Add remaining ingredients. Add additional water if needed to cover vegetables. Cook on high 3 hours. Cook on low, additional 5-6 hours or until vegetables are tender.

CHICKEN NOODLE SOUP

Use chicken vegetable recipe. Last ½ hour of cooking add ½ pkg. egg noodles.

COLD SHRIMP SOUP

1 quart clamato juice
½ cup chopped cucumber, peeled
1/3 cup chopped green onion
4 oz. salad shrimp
2 tbs. oil
2 tbs. red wine vinegar
2 tsp. sugar
1 tsp. dill weed
1 clove garlic, crushed
3 oz. cream cheese, cubed
1 avocado, peeled and diced
¼ tsp Tabasco

Mix all ingredients together. Chill and serve.

JAMBALAYA

½ lb. cooked smoked sausage, halved and sliced
2 cups cooked ham, chunked
1 lb. cooked shrimp, peeled and deveined
¼ cup oil
1 lg. oil
1 lg. onion
5 green onions, chopped
2 cloves garlic, minced
2 celery ribs, chopped
1 bell pepper, chopped
1 can (14-1/2 oz.) diced tomatoes, do not drain
4 cups chicken broth
1 cup cooked rice
4 tsp. Worcestershire sauce
1 tsp. creole
½ tsp. pepper
1 tsp. dried thyme (optional)
½ tsp. garlic
1/8 tsp. cayenne pepper

Saute onion, garlic, green pepper, & celery in oil. Drain off oil. Add all ingredients to crock pot. Cook on high 2 hours. Cook on low, for additional 4 hours or until heated through. Also, can be cooked in a Dutch oven. Heat through and serve immediately.

SANDWICH SECTION

While living in Illinois I worked at a small farmer's bank located in Wyanet. As a franchise bank we had to interact with other banks in the area. With constant expansion, more duties and responsibilities were thrown in my lap. Often I would call Pam at the Princeton branch for her knowledge and assistance. She was always very kind and helpful. Even though we had met at bank meetings our schedules never allowed us to speak outside of banking. As time passed we became phone buddies. After a period of time we decided to meet at a tea room for lunch. On the menu there was a cucumber sandwich which I ordered and thought was delicious. I later created a recipe for this sandwich which is still a favorite of mine today. Over the years we had many fine lunches and excellent conversations. I left Wyanet almost a decade ago, however, Pam and I still remain friends. Since, we have both been through divorces, have remarried and have been blessed with beautiful grandchildren. Through these times, her friendship has meant a great deal to me. If there is someone out there you want to get to know better, invite them to lunch for a sandwich. It may turn into something wonderful.
(Cucumber Sandwich)

FRENCH DIP

1 – 5-6 lb. round or rump roast
1 tsp. garlic powder
1 tsp pepper
1 tsp. salt
2 pkgs. Aujus Mix
1 pkg. hoagie rolls
Sauté onion & pepper on the side (optional)

Season roast well with garlic salt and pepper. Place in large roasting pan. Add 1 cup water. Cover. Bake at 350 for 2 hours. Remove and cool to handle. Save juices. Slice meat thin. Place back in juices and add 2 pkgs. Aujus (mix as directed) Place back in oven for 30 minutes or until meat is good and tender. Add additional water to broth if needed. Serve on hoagie rolls with a small bowl with juices for dipping.

Note: I like having a pan of sautéed onions and a pan of sautéed peppers on the side to put on the sandwich as desired.

BBQ SANDWICHES

2-1/2 lb, ground beef or leftover cooked pork (chopped)
1 onion, chopped
1-1/2 tsp. salt
¾ tsp. pepper
½ tbs. chili powder
3 tbs. Worcestershire sauce
3 tsp. prepared mustard
3 cups ketchup
8 tsp. brown sugar
1-1/2 tbs. cider vinegar
2 tbs. molasses or dark karo
Hamburger buns or rolls

Brown beef with onion and drain grease. Add remaining ingredients except buns. Mix well. Simmer 10 minutes. Serve on buns.

HAMBURGERS

1 lb. lean ground beef
Dash of pepper
Dash of salt
Dash of garlic powder
Hamburger buns or fresh sliced bread

Mix all ingredients and make into patties. If you are using hamburger buns make them round. If you are using bread slices, make them square. Set aside.

1 lg. tomato, sliced round
1 medium onion, sliced round
4-6 lettuce leaves
4 slices of cheese, American or Swiss, (optional)
Pickles (optional)

Slice tomato and onion. Place on a serving plate. Keep refrigerated while cooking burgers. For the best flavor burgers, cook on the grill (gas or charcoal) or cook in lg. frying pan over medium heat until browned on both sides. Serve with sliced tomato tray and choice of ketchup, mustard, mayo, etc.

CUCUMBER SANDWICH (A Summer Favorite)

Fresh sliced white bread
1 medium cucumber (peeled or not peeled)
Small block of havarti cheese
Dash of dill weed
Salt and pepper to taste
Mayonnaise or salad dressing

Slice cucumbers and cheese into thin pcs. (not to thin) Spread mayo on bread slices. Layer with cucumber and cheese slices. Sprinkle with dill. Salt and pepper to taste.

TUNA SALAD SANDWICH

1 can (6 oz.) water packed Tuna, drained & flaked
2/3 cup finely chopped celery or finely chopped cucumber
½ cup shredded carrot (optional)
¼ cup finely chopped green onions
2 tbs. Dijon mustard or regular mustard
3 tbs. sour cream
¼ cup mayonnaise or salad dressing
1 tbs. lemon juice
Salt & pepper to taste
8 slices of fresh bread (white, wheat, sourdough or rye) Fresh or Toasted
4 lg. lettuce leaves, halved
4 slices Swiss cheese (optional)

Mix all ingredients except bread and lettuce. Spread on bread. Top with lettuce and cheese.

RUEBEN SANDWICH (A favorite of mine & my husband)

12 oz. of thin or shaved pastrami meat
8 slices of Swiss cheese (deli style)
8 slices of rye bread
1 can (8 oz) Bavarian style sauerkraut
1 sm. onion cut in half & sliced thin
1 tbs. butter or margarine
8 tsp.. thousand island dressing
Margarine spread
Kosher pickle (optional)

Saute sliced onion in butter. Set aside. Drain and squeeze out sauerkraut. Set aside. Spread one side of each slice of rye with margarine. Place butter side down in large skillet. Spread 1 tsp. of thousand island dressing on each one. Place 1 slice of cheese over dressing. Top each with 3 oz. of pastrami. Layer desired amount of sauerkraut and sautéed onion. Top again with another slice of cheese. Top with buttered bread with 1 tsp. thousand island dressing, butter side out. Cook over medium heat until both sides are golden brown. Serve with a kosher pickle.

CARL'S EGG SANDWICH

Recipe for 1 sandwich:

2 slices of fresh white bread (toasted)
2 eggs cooked over well
Slice of cooked bacon (not crunchy)
1 slice of American cheese
Mayonnaise or salad dressing
Sweet relish (optional)
Salsa (optional)

Spread mayo on the toasted bread. Layer with egg, bacon and cheese. Top with slice of toasted bread. If using relish and salsa, place this on the cooked egg.

EGG SALAD SANDWICH

8 slices fresh white or wheat bread
8 hardboiled eggs, peeled and mashed
¼ of a medium onion or (1 very small) minced
¼ cup minced celery
2 tbs. sweet relish (optional)
½ tsp. mustard
Salt and pepper to taste
Mayonnaise or salad dressing

Mix in bowl, eggs, onion, celery, relish, mustard, salt and pepper. Mix enough mayonnaise for desired texture, starting with 2 tbs. Spread on bread slices.

DELI SANDWICH

Hoagie rolls
1 lb. lunchmeat (any style) or mix it up
Sliced cheese (any kind)
Sliced platter of tomatoes, onions, lettuce, pickles or any vegetables of your choosing.
Mayonnaise or salad dressing or choice of sandwich spread

This sandwich can be a lot of fun to make and to eat. Put all your favorite meats, cheeses, vegetables and salad spreads. Create your own original deli sandwich.

SALADS
&
DRESSINGS

Living in Brookings, Oregon, I was fortunate to make several close friends. As a real estate agent I met Bill and Alice looking for property in hopes of moving to Brookings. Eventually, they did move into town and Bill became an agent himself while Alice worked at the local bank. Our friendship grew which included many times when we would take turns hosting dinner parties. Larry and Helen, mutual friends, would also join us. Alice always cooked me under the table. One of my favorite dishes of hers was a spaghetti salad. Some of us have moved away from Brookings but continue to talk a few times a year. I know some day we will meet again for one of Alice's delicious meals. Betty Lou and her husband Milt were clients of mine. Betty Lou is one of the sweetest ladies you could ever meet. We became and have remained friends. I will never forget our special lunches out, sharing good conversation over soup and salad. I feel fortunate to have met so many special people in my life. (Spaghetti Salad)

COLESLAW

1 pkg. (16 oz.) coleslaw mix or 3-4 cups shredded cabbage & 1 cup shredded carrots
1 cup finely chopped bell pepper
½ cup mayonnaise or salad dressing
¼ cup lemon juice
2 tbs. sugar
1 tbs. prepared mustard
1 tsp. celery seed
1 tsp. salt

Mix mayo, lemon juice, sugar, mustard, celery seed and salt. Pour over cabbage mix and toss. Chill for 2 hours.

ORIENTAL SLAW   (A favorite at our pig roasts)

1 lb. coleslaw mix
2 bunches of green onions, chopped
1 cup toasted slivered almonds
1 cup sunflower seeds
2 pkg. oriental flavor ramen noodles, crumbled
1 pkg. seasoning from ramen noodles
¾ cup oil
½ cup sugar
1/3 cup vinegar

Mix 1 pkg. seasoning from ramen noodles with oil, sugar and vinegar. Pour over slaw mix, crumbled noodles, onion, sunflower seeds and almonds. Toss. Chill for 2 hours.

AMANDA'S PEA SALAD

3 cans peas, drained (put in freezer until firm but not frozen
1 (8oz.) block of cheddar cheese, cubed
½ onion, chopped
3-4 hard boiled eggs, peeled and chopped
1 cup mayonnaise

Fold all ingredients together. Chill until served.

ORIENTAL PASTA SALAD

2 cups elbow macaroni, cooked to directions, rinsed in cold water & drained
2 carrots , cut into 1 in. strips
1 cup snow peas, halved
2 green onions, chopped
½ cup sweet red pepper, thinly sliced

Dressing:

½ cup mayonnaise
½ cup sour cream
1 tbs. cider or red wine vinegar
1 tbs. soy sauce
½ tsp. ground ginger
¼ tsp. pepper

Add carrots, peas, onion and red pepper to cooked macaroni. In a sm. bowl, whisk dressing ingredients. Pour over salad and toss. Chill for 2 hours.

SALAMI & SHELLS SALAD

7 oz. pasta shells, cooked to directions, rinsed in cold water & drained
1 cup halved cherry tomatoes
1 cup halved black olives
6 oz. mozzarella, cut in small chunks
4 oz. salami, cut in small chunks
½ cup green pepper, chopped
4 green onion, chopped

Dressing:

1/3 cup oil
3 tbs. cider or red wine vinegar
1 tsp. salt
1 tsp. basil
½ tsp. dried oregano (optional)
¼ tsp. garlic powder

Mix dressing ingredients. Mix well. Toss pasta , vegetables, cheese and salami. Pour dressing over salad. Chill until serving.

PENNE SALAD

1 lb. penne pasta, cooked to directions, rinsed in cold water & drained
3 lg. peppers, green, yellow, & red, cut in strips
4 lg. ripe tomatoes, chopped
½ cup green onion, chopped

Dressing:

1 tbs. Dijon mustard
5 tbs. red wine vinegar
1 lg. clove garlic, crushed
4 tbs. lemon juice
2 tsp. sugar
½ tsp. pepper
½ cup olive oil
¼ cup Italian dressing
2 tbs. fresh basil chopped or ½ tsp. dry basil

Mix dressing ingredients together. Mix pasta and vegetables together. Pour dressing over pasta and toss. Refrigerate for several hours.

ITALIAN PASTA SALAD

16 oz. shell pasta, cooked to directions, rinsed in cold water and drained
¼ lb. hard salami, cubed
¼ lb. sliced pepperoni, halved
4 oz. provolone cheese, cubed
4 tomatoes, chopped
½ cup stuffed pimento/green olives, sliced
½ cup black olives, sliced
½ tsp. pepper
1 tsp. dried oregano
1 bottle (8 oz.) Italian salad dressing

Toss all ingredients together and chill.

ANTIPASTO SALAD

16 oz. rotini pasta, cooked to directions, rinsed in cold water & drained
15 oz. can garbanzo beans, rinsed and drained
3-1/2 oz. sliced pepperoni, halved
1 can (2-1/4 oz) black olives, drained and sliced
½ cup sweet red pepper, chopped
½ cup bell pepper, chopped
4 mushrooms, sliced
2 garlic cloves, minced
2 tsp. dried basil or 2 tbs. fresh minced basil
2 tsp. salt
½ tsp. oregano or 1-1/2 fresh minced oregano
½ tsp. pepper
¼ tsp. cayenne pepper
1 cup olive oil or vegetable oil
2/3 cup lemon juice

Mix seasonings, oil and lemon juice. Mix remaining ingredients for salad. Toss oil dressing into salad. Refrigerate overnight or chill for at least 6 hours.

DILLY PASTA SALAD

2-3/4 cup shell pasta, cooked to directions, rinsed in cold water& drained
1 cup cherry tomatoes, halved
1 cup green pepper, sliced thin
1 cup shredded cheddar cheese
½ cup green onion, chopped
½ cup black olives, sliced

Dressing:

¼ cup olive oil or vegetable oil
2 tbs. lemon juice
2 tbs. white wine vinegar or cider vinegar
1 tsp. dill weed
1 tsp. dried oregano
1 tsp salt
1/8 tsp. pepper

Mix salad ingredients together. Mix dressing ingredients together. Pour dressing over salad and toss. Chill

JALAPENO SLAW

1 pkg. shredded coleslaw mix
1 lg. tomato, seeded and chopped
4 green onions, chopped
2 jalapeno peppers, finely chopped
1/8 cup cider vinegar
3 tbs. honey
½ tsp. salt

Mix all ingredients. Chill for 2 hours.

24 HOUR SALAD (I rate this Excellent)

1 head lettuce, chopped or torn
1 tbs. sugar
6 hard boiled eggs, peeled and sliced
1 (10 oz.) frozen peas, thawed
1 lb. bacon, cooked crisp, drain & crumble
1 cup shredded swiss cheese
1 cup mayonnaise or salad dressing

Layer in a large bowl as follows: Lettuce, sugar, eggs, peas, bacon (cooled), cheese. Seal with mayo. Refrigerate overnight. Mix and serve.

PEACHY CHICKEN SALAD

4 cups sm. pasta shells, cooked as directed
¾ lb. cooked cubed chicken
½ cup dried peaches or apricots, cut in tiny pieces
¼ cup dried sweetened cranberries, chopped
3 oz. real bacon bits
2 tbs. fresh chives, chopped (optional)
1-1/4 cup peach or apricot syrup

Mix all ingredients together. Chill before serving.

TACO SALAD

8 flour tortillas
3 bacon strips
1 lb. ground beef
2 onions, chopped
2 cloves of garlic, minced
3 tbs. chili powder
1 tsp. salt
1 tsp. cumin
1 can (14 oz.) diced tomatoes, Do not drain
1 can (16 oz.) refried beans (optional)
1 head lettuce shredded
Toppings: sour cream, guacamole, salsa, (optional)

Butter 1 side of each tortilla. Place in greased round 1 qt. casserole dish. Press down to make a tortilla bowl. Bake at 375 until browned. Set aside. Cook bacon until crisp. Remove and crumble. Cook beef in bacon grease. When done, drain grease. Add bacon, onion, garlic, and seasonings. Simmer until onions are tender. Stir in tomatoes and refried beans.
Place shredded lettuce in each tortilla bowl. Place meat mixture over lettuce. Top with choice of toppings.

POTATO SALAD

8-9 potatoes, peeled and cubed, boiled until tender, drained and cooled
2 ribs celery, diced
1 med. onion, chopped
1 tbs. prepared mustard
5 hard boiled eggs, peeled and chopped
1 tsp. paprika
1 tsp. salt
½ tsp. pepper
½ cup sweet pickle relish
¾ to 1 cup mayonnaise or salad dressing
¼ tsp. celery salt

After potatoes have cooled add remaining ingredients except mayo. Mix gently. Add enough mayo for right consistency. Do not over mix. Chill 2-3 hours before serving.

SPINACH SALAD

Washed torn spinach (8-9 cups)
1 can (15 oz.) mandarin oranges, drained & chilled
1-1/2 cup fresh sliced mushrooms
1 sm. red onion, sliced in thin strips
3 boiled eggs, peeled and crumbled

Dressing:

¼ cup orange juice
3 tbs. red wine vinegar
2 tbs. sugar
1 tbs. oil
1 tsp. grated orange peel
1 tsp. poppy seeds
¼ tsp. salt

Combine salad ingredients. Chill. Mix dressing ingredients. Chill. Pour dressing over spinach mixture just before serving.

CHESTNUT PEA SALAD

2 carrots, chopped
1 pkg. (16 oz.) frozen peas, thawed
1 can (8 oz.) sliced water chestnuts, drained
2 green onions, chopped
½ cup mozzarella cheese, shredded
5 pc. bacon cooked and crumbled or 5 tbs. real bacon bits
¼ tsp. pepper
½ cup Ranch dressing

Boil carrots until tender. Drain and rinse in cold water. Add peas, chestnuts, onions and cheese. Set aside. Combine ranch dressing, bacon and pepper. Pour over salad. Chill until served.

SPAGHETTI SALAD

4 oz. spaghetti, broken in thirds, cooked to directions, rinsed & drained
½ cup oil
¼ cup red wine vinegar
1 lg. clove garlic, crushed
¼ tsp. dried basil
¼ tsp. salt
1/8 tsp. pepper
1 – 6 oz. jar marinated artichoke hearts, drained & chopped
1 cup fresh mushrooms, sliced
2 tomatoes, peeled, seeded and chopped
¼ cup walnuts, chopped & toasted
2 tbs. parsley

Combine cooked spaghetti, artichoke hearts, tomatoes, walnuts & mushrooms.
Mix other ingredients together. Mix well. Toss into spaghetti. Chill.

CUCUMBER SALAD

4-5 cucumbers, peeled and sliced
1 bunch green onion, chopped
¼ cup evaporated milk
½ cup sugar
¼ tsp. garlic salt
¼ tsp. onion salt
1 tbs. parsley
Salt and pepper to taste
1 cup mayonnaise or salad dressing

Mix together. Chill for several hours.

WEIGHT WATCHERS SALAD

3-4 med. apples, peeled and diced
2-3 carrots, peeled and diced
1 cup raisins
½ cup walnuts, chopped
1 cup low fat mayonnaise

Mix together. Chill for 1 hour. Note: If you are not watching your weight; use 1 cup regular mayonnaise or salad dressing.

PISTACHIO SALAD

1 box Instant pistachio pudding
1 can sweetened pineapple chunks
1 carton cool whip
¼ cup nuts (pecans or almonds)
1 cup mini marshmallows

Mix well pudding mix and pineapple. Fold in remaining ingredients. Chill.

MANDARIN/CHICKEN SALAD

4 cups cooked cubed chicken
1 (20 oz) can pineapple chunks, drained
1 can (11 oz.) mandarin oranges, drained
1 cup chopped celery
1 cup mayonnaise or salad dressing
½ cup black olives, sliced (optional)
½ cup green pepper, chopped
2 tbs. grated onion
1 tbs. prepared mustard
¼ tsp. salt
1/8 tsp. pepper
1 can (5 oz.) chow mein noodles

Combine all ingredients except noodles. Mix. Serve over chow mein noodles.

THREE BEAN SALAD

1 can each of green beans, waxed beans & kidney beans, drained
¼ cup chopped onion
2 cloves of garlic, minced
1 tbs. parsley flakes
½ cup Italian salad dressing

Mix all ingredients. Chill before serving.

APPLE SALAD

1 lg. golden apple, diced
1 lg. red apple, diced
1 tsp. lemon juice
1 can (20 oz.) pineapple chucks, drained
1 cup mini marshmallows
2/3 cup flaked coconut
½ cup walnuts, chopped
¼ cup raisins
¼ cup mayonnaise or salad dressing
2 tbs. minced celery

Toss apples and lemon juice. Add remaining ingredients. Mix well. Chill for 1 hour.

CREAMY MARSHMALLOW SALAD

1 bag mini marshmallows
1 pkg. lime jello
½ pkg. flaked coconut
½ cup sliced almonds
1container sour cream (16 oz.)
1 lg. can pineapple chucks, drained
1 can fruit cocktail, drained

Mix together. Chill

CHERRY COLA SALAD

¾ cup sugar
¾ cup water
1 can (21 oz) cherry pie filling
2 – 3oz. pkg. cherry jello
1 can (20 oz.) crushed pineapple
½ can cola
1 tbs. lemon juice
½ cup walnuts, chopped (optional)

Heat to boil, sugar and water. Add pie filling and boil again. Pour in jello to dissolve. Add remaining ingredients. Mix. Chill

HELPFUL HINTS FOR MAKING DRESSING;

Keep a 1 quart jar with a lid on hand. Use this to mix and shake and store dressings.

FRENCH DRESSING;

1 tbs. Dijon mustard
1 tbs. minced onion
3 tbs. cider or white vinegar
½ cup olive oil or vegetable oil

Mix in jar, shake well & chill.

WESTERN FRENCH DRESSING

1 cup oil
1/3 cup red wine vinegar
2/3 cup catsup
2/3 cup sugar
1 tbs. Worcestershire
1 tsp. salt
1 clove garlic, crushed
1 sm. onion minced

Mix in jar, shake well & chill.

OIL & VINEGAR DRESSING

1-1/2 cups sugar
1 tbs. ground mustard
1 tsp. salt
½ tsp. pepper
½ tsp. paprika
½ cup hot water
¼ cup vinegar
2 garlic cloves, halved
¼ cup oil

Mix in jar, shake well, Refrigerate for 2-3 hours. Remove garlic before serving.

BLUE CHEESE DRESSING

1-1/2 cup mayonnaise
½ cup sour cream
¼ cup cider vinegar
4 tsp. sugar
½ tsp. dry mustard
½ tsp. garlic powder
½ tsp. onion powder
1 pkg. (4 oz.) blue cheese, crumbled

In a bowl, combine all ingredients except cheese. Mix well. Stir in bleu cheese. Cover and refrigerate for 2-3 hours.

HONEY MUSTARD DRESSING

1-1/4 cup mayonnaise
1/3 cup honey
2/3 cup oil
1 tbs. vinegar
2 tbs. parsley flakes
2 tbs. prepared mustard
1 tsp. onion flakes

Mix in jar, shake well, refrigerate before serving.

CREAMY DIJON DRESSING

1 cup buttermilk
8 (oz.) sour cream
1/3 cup parmesan, grated
1 tbs. Dijon style mustard
1 tsp. lemon juice
¼ tsp. pepper

Mix in jar. Shake well. (or whip with mixer or food processor). Chill.

BUTTERMILK DRESSING

1/2 cup buttermilk
2 tbs. cider vinegar
¼ cup oil
½ tsp. salt
1/8 tsp. pepper
¼ tsp. celery seed
1/8 tsp. Worcestershire
2-3 drops Tabasco (optional)

Mix in jar. Shake well. Refrigerate until serving.

CUCUMBER/BUTTERMILK DRESSING

1 cucumber, seeded and finely chopped
1-1/2 cups buttermilk
1 clove garlic, crushed
½ tsp. salt
¼ cup red wine vinegar
2 tsp. prepared horseradish
1 tsp. dill weed
1 tsp. paprika

Blend with mixer or processor. Chill until serving

VINAIGRETTE DRESSING

¼ cup red wine vinegar
½ cup water
¼ tsp. garlic powder
¼ tsp. onion powder
1 tsp. lemon juice
1 tsp. soy sauce
½ tsp. Dijon style mustard
Dash of cayenne pepper

Mix in jar, Shake well. Refrigerate until served.

Note: For Citrus Vinaigrette, omit soy sauce and pepper. Add 1 tsp. brown sugar and 1 lg. orange squeezed.

CRANBERRY VINAIGRETTE DRESSING

1 cups raspberries, juiced (discard seeds)
½ cup cranberry juice
½ cup red wine vinegar
¼ cup hot water
1 tbs. oil
½ tsp salt
1 tbs. sugar

Blend with mixer or processor until smooth. Chill

RUSSIAN DRESSING

½ cup mayonnaise or salad dressing
½ cup plain yogurt
2 tbs. chili sauce
2 tbs. pickle relish
2 tbs. sweet red pepper, minced

In a bowl, whisk together. Chill.

TOMATO/BASIL DRESSING

1 tomato, peeled, seeded and chopped
½ sweet red pepper, chopped
1/3 cup fresh basil leaves or 2 tbs. dried basil
1 clove garlic
2 tbs. white vinegar
1 tbs. tomato paste
1 tsp. sugar
¼ tsp. salt
1/8 tsp. pepper
1/3 cup mayonnaise or salad dressing

Blend together. Chill

RASPBERRY DRESSING

1 cup oil
½ cup sugar
1/3 cup raspberry vinegar
1 tsp. salt
1 tsp. dry mustard
1-1/2 tsp. poppy seeds

Mix in jar. Shake well. Refrigerate until serving

Note: If you have fresh raspberries. Use ½ cup fresh (blended) and 2 tbs. red wine vinegar.

This is a great dressing served over fresh spinach and strawberries.

HONEY/CANTALOUPE DRESSING

1 cup chopped cantaloupe, blended until smooth
½ cup vanilla yogurt
1 tbs. honey

Mix together. Chill until serving. Good over fruit salads.

BANANA DRESSING

1 ripe banana, mashed
1 cup sour cream
¼ cup sugar
1 tbs. poppy seeds
1 tbs. dry mustard
½ tsp salt

Blend together. Chill.

Good over fruit salads or salad greens with orange and grapefruit sections.

DIPS & SPREADS

McCrory, Arkansas is a small farming community with many life long residents. Most people living here knows everybody and news spreads quickly. This is where my husband was born and raised. When I moved here several years ago I did not know anyone else. All my family and friends lived far away. We were busy developing a parcel of property and expanding our business so there was not much time to meet people. A regular stop was to the local post office. Here worked a nice, attractive lady named Marilyn. She was always very kind and helpful. The first Christmas rolled around on our new property and to my surprise there was a knock at the door and it was Marilyn. There she stood with this big cheese ball in hand. What a wonderful unexpected surprise. How sweet of her to bring us this special gift. As soon as she left , out came the crackers and WOW it was delicious. Since then over the holidays I try and treat her to something from my kitchen. Due to our conflicting schedules we rarely get to visit but her kindness with never be forgotten. (Cheese Ball)

VEGETABLE DIP

1 pkg. (8 oz.) cream cheese, softened
1 tbs. mayonnaise or salad dressing
1 tbs. lemon juice
½ tsp. salt
1/8 tsp. pepper
¾ cup grated carrots
½ cup diced celery
½ cup diced cucumber
½ cup green pepper
1/3 cup diced green onions or ¼ cup minced onions

Beat cream cheese, mayo, lemon juice, salt and pepper until smooth. Stir in vegetables. Refrigerate for 2-3 hours. Serve with bread or crackers.

SPINACH DIP

1 envelope of vegetable soup mix
1 pint sour cream
½ cup mayo or salad dressing
½ tsp. lemon juice
1 pkg. (10 oz.) frozen spinach chopped, thawed & squeezed
1 can chopped and drained water chestnuts

Mix all together and chill. Serve with bread or crackers.

Note: Take a ½ loaf of French bread and hollow out carefully, saving center for bread servings. Place dip in center of loaf. Serve with bread pcs. or crackers around the loaf.

RADISH DIP

1 cup plain yogurt
1 cup chopped radishes (13)
1/3 cup mayo or salad dressing
¼ tsp. hot sauce
1/8 tsp. pepper

Mix all together. Chill. Serve with raw vegetables.

DILL DIP

1 cup sour cream
1 cup mayonnaise
1-1/2 tbs. chopped parsley
1-1.2 tbs. minced onion
½ tsp. dill weed
½ tsp. Beau-Monde (seasoning)
½ tsp. garlic salt

Blend all ingredients together. Chill for 12 hours. Serve with raw vegetables.

TACO DIP

½ lb. hamburger
1 med. onion finely chopped
1 pkg. (1-1/4 oz) taco seasoning
1 can (6 oz.) tomato paste
1 sm. can tomato sauce
1 tbs. sugar
1 sm. can chopped black olives
2 tbs. hot sauce
Corn chips

Brown hamburger and onion. Drain grease. Mix with remaining ingredients. Simmer 10 minutes. Serve with corn chips.

CHILI CON QUESO

¾ cup onion
1/3 cup chopped green pepper
2 tbs. butter or margarine
1 pound processed cheese
1 can (4 oz.) pimentos with liquid
1 Tbs. chili powder
1 tsp/ garlic salt
Tortilla chips

Saute onion and green pepper in butter. Melt cheese with onion and peppers. Add pimentos with liquid. Stir well with chili powder and garlic salt. Serve with tortilla chips.

CRAB DIP

12 oz. of crab meat (I like to use imitation crab) chopped
1 cup sour cream
3 oz. cream cheese, softened
1 tsp. prepared horseradish
3 tbs. mayonnaise
2 tsp. lime juice
½ tsp. seasoned salt or creole
2 tsp. chopped chives
2 drops of Tabasco
Salt and pepper to taste

Drain crab. Blend sour cream into cream cheese. Mix in crab and seasonings. Mix thoroughly. Chill overnight. Serve with crackers.

SHRIMP PATE'

1 pound cream cheese
1-1/2 tbs. lemon juice
1 tsp. sugar
1 pound salad shrimp, drained
1 tbs. chopped parsley
1 dash vermouth
3 med. green onions chopped
1 tsp. grey poupon mustard
Salt and pepper to taste

With mixer whip cream cheese and half of shrimp. Whip until shrimp are broken. Fold in remaining ingredients. Chill thoroughly. Serve with crackers.

MEXICAN EGG SPREAD

6 hard boiled eggs
1 med. tomato, finely chopped
3 green onions, chopped or 1 tsp. onion powder
¼ cup mayonnaise or salad dressing
½ of a pkg. of taco seasoning
½ cup sour cream
½ cup avocado (optional)

Peel and finely chop eggs. Combine eggs with tomato, onions, mayonnaise and taco seasoning. Place egg mixture in serving bowl. Chill. Top with sour cream and avocado.

CHEESE BALL (A Favorite in our Family)

2 pkg. cream cheese
1 pkg. shredded sharp cheddar cheese
3 tbs. lemon juice
3 tbs. Worcestershire
¾ cup chopped green onion
¼ cup chopped bell pepper
1 jalapeno chopped fine
1 pkg. chopped pecans (about 6 oz.)

Mix all ingredients, except pecans. Roll into ball. Roll ball in pecans. Place in serving bowl. Serve with crackers.

GRAVY
SAUCES
&
BRINES

Some of my earliest memories are when mom and grandpa would go deer hunting.
It was a family project to help cut the meat down and package it up. All the extra
pieces got put into jerky which my mom dried in the oven. This was my favorite
part of the deer. As my boys grew into teens they began deer and elk hunting. When
we were lucky enough to get a deer it was processed into pepperoni sticks and jerky.
We shared with our friends and family but my sons were like little squirrels hording
it all away in their rooms for a rainy day. (Jerky Brine)

SAUSAGE GRAVY

1 pound pork sausage
2 tbs. finely chopped onion
6 tbs. flour
1 quart milk
Dash of hot sauce
Dash of Worcestershire sauce
Salt & Pepper to taste

Brown sausage, add onion until cooked. Drain grease. Mix flour into sausage. Add milk and seasonings. Cook until thickens, constantly stirring.

BROWN GRAVY

¼ cup flour
1-1/2 cups beef drippings or broth
½ cup water
½ cup dry red wine (optional)
¼ tsp. ground red pepper
¼ tsp. pepper
Salt to taste

Whisk all ingredients (except wine).
Note: I use a glass jar with a lid and I shake vigorously.

Cook over medium heat, stirring constantly until thickens. If using the wine: Boil wine & add to thickened gravy.

CHICKEN or TURKEY GRAVY

1 – 10 ½ oz. chicken broth or drippings
½ cup milk
2 tbs. butter or margarine (if using broth) (not needed if using drippings)
2 tbs. flour
2 tsp dried minced onion (optional)
1/8 tsp. pepper

Melt butter. Whisk all ingredients (or shake vigorously in a jar) Cook over medium heat until thickens.

Note: Add additional flour if needed to make thicker. Do not add to hot mixture. Whisk flour with small amount of cold milk. This will eliminate clumps of flour in the gravy.

HOLLANDAISE SAUCE

3 lg. egg yolks
1 tbs. lemon juice
½ cup stick butter

Stir yolks and lemon juice vigorously in saucepan. Add ¼ cup butter. Whisk over very low heat until melted. Add remaining butter. Continue stirring vigorously until butter is melted and sauce thickens.

Note: Use very low heat so the eggs have time to cook without curdling.

SWEET AND SOUR SAUCE

1/3 cup sugar
1/3 cup cider vinegar
¼ cup catsup
2 tbs. soy sauce
2 tbs. dry sherry
2 tbs. cornstarch
½ cup pineapple juice

Combine first 5 ingredients in a saucepan. Dissolve cornstarch in pineapple juice. Add to sugar mixture. Bring to boil. Stir constantly. Cook one minute or until thickened.

FAJITA MARINADE

½ cup Italian salad dressing
½ cup salsa
1 tsp. shredded lime peel
2 tbs. lime juice
1 tbs. fresh snipped cilantro or 1 tsp. dry cilantro
¼ tsp hot sauce

Mix all ingredients. Marinade meat for at least 4 hours or overnight. Boil reserve marinade to serve with Fajitas.

ALFREDO SAUCE

1   8oz. pkg. cream cheese
½ cup milk
¼ cup parmesan cheese
¼ cup butter
Garlic powder to taste

Melt cream cheese, milk and butter in a saucepan over medium heat. Add parmesan cheese. Whisk. Add garlic to taste.

WHITE SAUCE

2 tbs. margarine or butter
2 tbs. flour
1 cup milk
¼ tsp. salt
1/8 tsp. pepper

Melt margarine. Stir in flour, salt and pepper. Cook until smooth. Remove from heat. Gradually stir in milk. Heat to boiling, stirring constantly for 1 minute.

Note: Thick White Sauce; Increase margarine to ¼ cup and four to ¼ cup
        Thin White Sauce; Decrease margarine to 1 tbs. and flour to 1 tbs.

CHEESE SAUCE

White sauce recipe: Add ¼ tsp dry mustard to flour & ½ cup cheddar cheese to sauce until melted.

DILL SAUCE

White sauce recipe: Add 1 tsp. fresh chopped dill or ½ tsp. dried dill weed and dash of nutmeg to flour.

MUSTARD SAUCE

White sauce recipe: Decrease margarine to 1 tbs. & flour to 1 tbs. After boiling sauce, stir in 3 tbs. mustard & 1 tbs. horseradish.

JERKY BRINE

Brine for Beef, Deer, or Elk Jerky:
1/3 cup sugar
¼ cup salt
2 cups soy sauce
1 cup water
1 cup dark red wine
½ tsp onion powder
½ tsp. pepper
½ tsp. garlic powder
½ tsp. Tabasco or hot sauce

Mix all ingredients. Let jerky sliced meat sit in brine for at least 8 hours. Do not rinse, air dry. Ready to smoke or dehydrate.

Note: Hickory is the best flavor for the smoking process.

TERIYAKI SAUCE

1 cup soy sauce
¼ cup packed brown sugar
2 tbs. lemon juice
1 tsp. ground ginger
½ tsp. garlic powder
¼ tsp. onion powder

Mix all ingredients until sugar dissolves. If using as a marinade, let stand in jar or covered dish overnight.

PIZZA SAUCE

½ cup olive oil
¼ cup minced garlic
1 sm. can tomato paste
1 medium can tomato sauce or 2 sm. cans
¼ cup minced fresh basil or 1 tbs. dry
¼ cup minced fresh oregano or 1 tbs. dry
1 tbs. salt
¼ cup minced fresh parsley or 1 tbs. dry
½ tsp pepper

Mix all ingredients. Bring to boil, stir constantly, simmer 5 minutes & cool.

EASY BARBECUE SAUCE

1 cup catsup
½ cup wine vinegar
1 tsp. Worcestershire sauce
1 tsp. instant minced onion or ¼ minced fresh onion
½ tsp. creole or season salt
¼ tsp. garlic salt or 1/8 tsp. garlic powder & ¼ tsp. salt
1/8 tsp. pepper

Combine all ingredients and mix well. Use as a marinade or BBQ sauce.

GARLIC BBQ SAUCE

1/2 cup salad oil
1/2 cup olive oil
4 tbs. catsup
5 cloves garlic pressed
½ tsp rosemary
3 tbs. red wine vinegar
1 tsp. oregano
1 tsp. salt
1 tsp. pepper
¼ cup lemon juice
1 tsp. Tabasco sauce
1 tsp Worcestershire sauce

Blend all ingredients together. Set for at least 1 hour. Better if sits over night in refrigerator. Use as a marinade or BBQ sauce.

SPAGHETTI SAUCE

2 tbs. olive oil or oil
1 onion minced
1 bell pepper chopped fine
2 cloves of garlic
1 cup red wine (optional)
1tbs. parsley
1 tsp. salt
1 tsp. basil
1 tbs. oregano
1 tsp. thyme (optional)
¼ tsp. crushed red pepper
¼ tsp. black pepper
3/4 cup sugar
1 – can stewed tomatoes
1 (14 oz.) tomato sauce
2 cans tomato soup
1 cup water
1 sm. can mushrooms (optional) or 1 cup fresh sliced

Heat oil. Saute onion, bell pepper, garlic, and mushrooms until tender. Mix all other ingredients. Simmer on low for 20-30 minutes, stirring occasionally.

MEAT SAUCE

Use Spaghetti sauce recipe. After onion sauté add cooked meat and sauté additional 3 minutes. Add to remaining ingredients.

Note: Sauce is always better after sitting for 24 hours in refrigerator.

BEEF

On my son's birthdays I would ask them what they wanted for their birthday dinner. It never seemed to change. Carl wanted burritos and Alan wanted tacos or chili dogs. I don't think neither remembered from year to year what their presents were or what the cake looked like but they always seem to remember their birthday dinners. It touches me that my sons continue to share their childhood memories with me. It's amazing how the simplest and least monetary things in life create the longest and most cherished thoughts. (Burritos)   (Tacos)

CROCK POT STEW

1-1/2 lb. stew meat, cut in 1 inch cubes
2 tsp. garlic, minced
1 cup flour
Cooking oil
1 tsp. salt
1 tsp. pepper
½ tsp. garlic powder
1 onions, chopped
6 carrots, sliced bite size
3-4 potatoes, peeled and cubed bite size
1 quart stewed tomatoes
1 cup celery, sliced bite size
1 tsp. celery salt
3 cups beef broth
Additional salt & pepper to taste

Mix flour, salt, pepper and garlic powder. Coat stew meat pcs. In a lg. frying pan, put enough oil to cover bottom of pan. On med. heat brown coated stew meat with minced garlic. Cook until browned. Spray crock pot with cooking spray. Place meat in crock pot. Add all remaining ingredients. Add additional water if needed to cover vegetables. Stir. Cook high for 3 hours. Turn to low for 4-5 hours until meat and vegetables are tender. If needed salt and pepper to taste.
Note: Use vegetables of your liking. Sometimes I add squash, eggplant, corn or okra. To thicken if needed: shake up 3 tbs. flour & ½ cup milk. Stir in stew.

BEEF MEDALLIONS

2 – (8 oz) strip steaks
2 tbs. brown mustard
2 tbs. shallots or green onions, minced
3 tbs. butter
2 tbs. brandy
2 tbs. dark red wine
1 dash Worcestershire
1 tsp. flaked parsley (optional)
Salt and pepper to taste

Pound steaks with a sharp edge of knife, both directions. Spread 1 tbs. mustard on 1 side of each steak. Sprinkle 1 tbs. shallots on each steak. Press on to adhere. Season with salt and pepper. Melt butter in skillet. Over med-high place steaks in butter and cook on both sides until well browned. Add brandy and light with match. Be careful doing this. When flames die down remove steaks to serving dish. Add wine and Worcestershire to skillet. Bring to boil scraping drippings from the cooked steak. Stir well. Pour juices over steak. Sprinkle with parsley if desired.

POT OF CHILI

2 lb. ground beef
Salt and pepper to taste
1 onion, chopped
1 bell pepper, chopped
1 cup celery, chopped
1 tsp. garlic, minced
2 pkg. chili seasoning mix (mild, medium or hot)
1 pint stewed tomatoes, drained
3-4 cans (8 oz) tomato sauce
1 can (15 oz) red beans, drained
1 can (15 oz) kidney beans, drained
1 can (15 oz) pinto beans, drained
1 cup shredded cheddar cheese (optional)

Brown hamburger with dash of salt and pepper. Drain grease. Add onion, bell pepper, celery and garlic. Saute until tender. In a lg. baking pot or Dutch oven put in 3 cans tomato sauce & remaining ingredients. If more sauce is needed to cover, add extra can of tomato sauce. Stir. Bake at 325 for 1 hour, stirring half way in cooking time. Sprinkle with shredded cheese. Serve with crackers.

Note: Extra chili in really good served over hamburgers, hotdogs and French fries.

TACOS

2 lb. ground beef
2 pkg. taco seasoning mix (mix water as directed)
2 tomatoes, chopped
1 lg. onion, chopped
2 bell peppers, chopped
1 pkg. shredded cheddar cheese
1 can (8 oz.) chopped black olive (optional)
Salsa (optional)
Sour cream (optional)
Hot sauce (optional)
1 pkg. (6 in.) flour tortillas or corn tortillas, warmed

Brown beef and add taco seasoning as directed. Heat and set aside keeping warm. Place chopped vegetables, cheese, salsa and sour cream in separate small dishes for serving. Serve beef on tortillas. Top with choice of toppings.

BEEF FAJITAS

1 lb. round steak, trimmed
1/3 cup lime juice
1 tsp. garlic salt
½ tsp. pepper
3 tbs. butter or margarine
4-6 flour tortillas

Pound steak into ¼ inch thickness. Cut across the grain into thin strips. Combine lime juice and seasonings. Pour over meat and cover. Refrigerate 8 hours or overnight. Drain marinade and discard. Pan fry butter and steak strips, (med-high heat) flipping until browned and tender. Serve over flour tortillas (warmed) with desired toppings.

Optional Toppings:

Shredded lettuce
Chopped tomato
Chopped green onions or onion
Chopped sweet peppers or bell pepper
Shredded cheese
Sour cream
Salsa

PRIME RIB (A Family Holiday Favorite)

8-10 lb. Prime Rib Roast
Salt
Horseradish crème (optional)

In morning remove roast from refrigerator. Place in roasting pan and generously rub salt on all sides. Let stand at room temperature for 2-4 hours. Pre-heat oven to 375. Place roast in oven (not covered) for 1 hour and 15 minutes. Do not open oven while cooking. (seal oven) Turn off oven. Leave roast in oven for 2-3 hours. Turn oven back on to 350 for 1 hour. Remove and cool 5-10 minutes. Serve immediately. End cuts will be well done. Center cuts will be rare. Serve with horseradish crème on the side.

Note: If you want the center cuts a little more done. After cooking 1 hour at 350, add ½ cup water to roasting pan. Cover roast tightly with foil and continue cooking for 40-50 minutes.

STUFFED PEPPERS

6 large bell peppers
1 lb. ground beef
1/8 cup chopped onion
1 cup cooked rice
1 tsp. salt
1 tsp garlic, mince
1 can tomato sauce (15 oz)
1-1/2 cups shredded mozzarella cheese

Leave the peppers whole. Cut the top out of each pepper, discarding the seeds and membrane. Rinse. Cook peppers in water (just to cover) at boiling for 5 minutes. Drain and set aside.
Cook beef and onion until browned. Drain off grease. Stir in rice, salt, garlic and 1 cup of tomato sauce. Cook until hot. Add ¾ cup cheese. Stir
Stuff the peppers with meat mixture. Stand upright in ungreased 8X8X2 baking dish. Pour remaining tomato sauce over peppers. Cover and bake at 350 for 45 minutes. Uncover for additional 10-15 minutes. Remove. Sprinkle remaining cheese over peppers.

CABBAGE ROLLS

Use same ingredients for stuff peppers
Use 12 cabbage leaves instead of peppers, following same steps for cooking.
Add 1 tsp. sugar and ½ tsp lemon juice to remaining tomato sauce.
Roll mixture up in cabbage leaves.

TACO CASSEROLE

2 lb. ground beef
1 bag taco chips or tortilla chips
1 can (10 oz) tomato sauce
1 can enchilada sauce (15 oz)
1 can refried beans (15 oz)
2 cups shredded cheddar cheese
2 cups mozzarella cheese
¼ cup sugar
Lettuce, salsa ,chopped black olives and sour cream (optional)
Crumble chips in a 9 X 13 baking pan. Brown beef and drain grease. Add tomato sauce, enchilada sauce and refried beans. Mix and pour over chips. Add cheddar cheese on top of meat, follow with mozzarella. Bake at 350 for 30 minutes. Let stand 5 minutes. Cut in Squares. Serve over lettuce with sour cream, salsa and chopped black olives.

MEAT LOAF

1-1/2 lb. ground beef
2 eggs
1/8 cup ketchup plus 1/8 cup ketchup for topping
1/8 cup salsa
1 tsp. salt
½ tsp. pepper
¼ cup crackers or bread crumbs
1 small onion, minced
1 tsp. flaked parsley
Dash of onion powder
Dash of celery salt
Dash of garlic powder
1 tbs. sugar

Mix all ingredients together in a large bowl. Mix well. Place in a greased casserole dish. Large enough to allow for grease cooking out. Bake (covered) at 350 for 30 minutes. Remove and drain grease. Place 1/8 cup ketchup over top. Reduce heat to 325. Cover and bake for another 30 minutes. Remove cover last 5 minutes of cooking.

MANICOTTI

1-1/2 lb. ground beef
½ cup onion, minced
2 cloves garlic, minced
½ tsp. pepper
½ tsp. season salt
¼ tsp. Italian seasoning
1 pkg. (10 oz) frozen spinach, thawed & squeezed
1 box Manicotti noodles, Partial pre-cook as directed on box
1 cup mozzarella cheese, shredded (optional)
1 jar (store bought) or 1 quart of (homemade) spaghetti sauce (meatless)
1/8 cup red wine (optional)

Brown beef, onion, garlic and seasonings. Drain grease. Mix with spinach and stuff manicotti shells full. Place manicotti in a greased shallow baking pan. Mix spaghetti sauce and wine. Cover with sauce. Bake covered at 350 for 35-40 minutes. Add cheese last 5-10 minutes of cooking.

BARBECUED SHORT RIBS

3-4 lb. beef short ribs
1-1/2 cups water
1 medium onion, sliced
1 tbs. cider vinegar

Sauce:
½ cup ketchup
¼ cup chopped onion
2 tbs. lemon juice
2 tsp minced garlic
2 tsp. sugar
½ tsp. salt
1/8 tsp. pepper

In a Dutch oven or lg. cooking pot, place ribs, water, onion and vinegar. Bring to a boil. Reduce heat and simmer for 1 hour, turning ribs occasionally. Drain. Place ribs in a ungreased 13X9X2 baking pan. Combine sauce ingredients and spoon over ribs. Cover and bake at 325 for 1 hour or until ribs are tender. Check ribs half way through. If drying add a little water to the pan.

BARBECUE BABY BACK RIBS

2-3 lb. ribs
Salt and pepper to taste

Basting Sauce:
3 tbs. butter melted
3 tbs. chili sauce
2 tbs. lemon juice
1/8 tsp. dry mustard
Dash of pepper

Combine basting ingredients. Rinse ribs and pat dry. Salt and pepper ribs. Baste ribs. Grill or (charcoal grill) ribs over medium heat turning until browned on both sides, (almost singed). Place ribs in lg. greased baking pan. Pour remaining sauce over ribs and 1/8 cup water to bottom of pan. Bake at 325 for 30-40 minutes (covered) or until ribs are tender.

Note: This basting sauce is also good on chicken and turkey legs.

PEPPER STEAK

1 lb boneless sirloin steak, cut in thin strips
Salt and pepper to taste
2 cups sweet pepper (red, yellow or green)
2 tbs. oil
1 medium onion, cut in thin strips
2 tsp. minced garlic
1 can mushroom soup
1 tbs. soy sauce
½ tsp. ground ginger
1 tsp. sugar
1 tbs. cornstarch
½ cup water
Cooked rice or noodles

In a lg. skillet heat 1 tbs. oil. Stir fry peppers, onion and garlic until crisp-tender. Remove and set aside. In same skillet add 1 tbs. oil and stir fry steak strips with salt and pepper to taste. Remove and set aside. In same skillet add and heat soup, soy sauce, ginger and sugar. Mix cornstarch and water in separate bowl. Add cornstarch to sauce and simmer until thickened, stirring constantly. Add steak strips and pepper/onion strips. Heat through, stirring often. Serve over cooked rice or noodles.

SWEET & SOUR BEEF (Crock Pot Dish)

2 lbs. boneless round steak, trimmed and cut in 1 inch cubes
2 tbs. oil
2 cans (8 oz) tomato sauce
2 cups thinly sliced carrots
2 cups pearl onions
1 bell pepper cut in 1 inch pcs.
½ cup molasses or dark karo
1/3 cup vinegar
¼ cup sugar
2 tsp. chili powder
2 tsp. paprika
1 tsp. salt
Cooked noodles

In a lg. skillet, brown steak in oil. Place in greased crock pot. Add remaining ingredients except the noodles. Mix, cover and cook on low for 7-8 hours or until meat is tender. Serve over noodles

ASIAN BEEF DISH

1 lb. boneless round steak, cut into 1X3 inch strips
1 jalapeno pepper, seeded and chopped fine
1 tbs. oil
1 pkg. (3 oz.) ramen noodles (beef flavor)
1 carrot, shredded
¼ cup steak sauce (any flavor)
2 tbs. green onion chopped
¼ cup chopped peanuts

Combine beef strips, jalapeno and oil in bowl. Toss to coat. Cook ramen noodles
without seasoning pack (reserve) as directed and drain. Cook beef in oil with
jalapeno. Stir fry until meat is no longer pink. Remove from skillet. Set aside. In
same skillet, combine cooked noodles, reserved seasoning pack, carrot, steak sauce
and green onion. Cook until hot. Add beef. Cook again until hot. Serve with peanuts
on top.

CORN BEEF HASH

1-1/2 cups cooked or canned corn beef, chopped
1 lg. pkg. frozen shredded hash browns, thawed
½ cup butter or margarine
½ cup green onion, chopped
½ cup sweet pepper, chopped
½ cup bell pepper, chopped (optional)
2 tsp. creole or season salt
¾ tsp. chili powder
Hot sauce (optional)

Cook hash browns with butter until tender in lg. frying pan. Add onion, peppers
and seasonings, except hot sauce. Cook again until hashbrowns turn golden brown.
Add corn beef. Stir and cook until hot. Sprinkle hot sauce to taste. Really good
served with eggs and toast.

HEARTY MEATBALLS (Really good served over rice)

1-1/2 lb. lean ground beef
1 egg, beaten
½ cup milk
1 tbs. cornstarch
1 med. onion, minced
1 tsp. salt
1/8 tsp. pepper
¼ tsp. ground nutmeg
¼ tsp. ground allspice
¼ tsp. ground ginger
4 tbs. butter or margarine

Gravy:
1 tbs. butter or margarine
2 tbs. flour
1 cup beef broth
½ cup milk

Mix meatball ingredients together, except butter. Shape into hearty size meatballs. Brown meatballs in butter, simmering until brown and cooked through. In a saucepan, mix gravy ingredients. Cook over med. heat stirring constantly until thickens. Remove meatballs from cooking pan draining excess grease. Pour gravy over meatballs. Serve over rice if desired.

MARINATED STEAK (For the grill)

2 lb. steak, 1 inch thickness
1-1/2 cups water
¾ cup soy sauce
¼ cup Worcestershire
1 med. onion, chopped
2 tbs. wine vinegar
2 tbs. lemon juice
2 tbs. brown mustard
2 tsp. minced garlic
1 tsp. Italian seasoning
1 tsp. pepper

Place steaks in a shallow pan or sealable plastic bag. Combine remaining ingredients. Mix well. Pour over steaks. Cover and refrigerate overnight. Remove meat, discarding marinade. Grill steaks over medium heat or coals, 6-8 minutes each side for rare. 8-10 minutes for medium and 11-13 minutes for well done.

SWEET & SOUR MEATBALLS (Appetizer)

1 lb. lean ground beef
1 cup soft bread crumbs
1 egg, slightly beaten
2 tbs. minced onion
2 tbs. milk
1 tsp. minced garlic
½ tsp. salt
1/8 tsp. pepper
1 tbs. oil

Sauce:
2/3 cup chili sauce
2/3 cup grape or currant jelly

Combine all ingredients except sauce ingredients.. Mix well. In a rounded tsp. size, form meatballs. (35-40 meatballs) Brown meatballs in oil at low heat. Drain off excess grease after browned. Mix chili sauce and jelly. Pour over meatballs. Simmer for 10 minutes or until sauce has thickened. Stir occasionally while simmering.

CRANBERRY MEATBALLS (Appetizer)

2 lb. lean ground beef
2 eggs, beaten
1 cup dry bread crumbs
1 tbs. parsley flakes
1/3 cup ketchup
2 tbs. minced onion
2 tbs. soy sauce
2 tsp. minced garlic
½ tsp. salt
¼ tsp. pepper
1 tbs. oil

Sauce:
1 can (16 oz) whole berry cranberry sauce
1 bottle chili sauce (12 oz)
1-1/2 tbs. brown sugar
1 tbs. prepared mustard
1 tbs. lemon juice
2 tsp. minced garlic

Follow same cooking instructions as the Sweet & Sour Meatball Recipe.

HAMBURGER CASSEROLE (Quick, Easy & Very Good)

1-1/2 lb. ground beef
1 medium onion, chopped
2 cans cream of mushroom soup
½ can evaporated milk
1 cup celery, chopped
1 – (4oz.) pkg. egg noodles
½ lb. processed cheese, cubed
Salt and pepper to taste

Fry meat,(salt and pepper to taste)onion and celery together until meat is browned. Drain Grease. Cook noodles as directed, drain. In a 13X9X2 greased baking dish. Add all ingredients. Stir. Cover and bake at 350 for 30 minutes.

HAMBURGER DELIGHT

1-1/2 lb ground beef
8 oz. egg noodles (cooked as directed)
¼ cup bell pepper, chopped (optional)
1 tsp. minced garlic
3 – (8 oz.) cans tomato sauce
1 tbs. sugar
¼ tsp. salt
¼ tsp. pepper
1 cup cottage cheese
1 – (8 oz.) pkg. cream cheese, softened
¼ cup sour cream
3 green onions, chopped
1 cup shredded cheddar cheese

Cook ground beef and garlic until browned. Drain. Add tomato sauce, sugar, salt and pepper. Stir noodles and meat mixture together. In a bowl combine cottage cheese, cream cheese, sour cream and onion. In a greased 13X9X2 baking pan place ½ noodle mixture. Top with cottage cheese mixture, spreading evenly. Place remaining noodles over cottage cheese mixture. Sprinkle with cheddar cheese. Cover and bake at 350 for 30 minutes or until heated through.

STROGANOFF

1 lb. ground beef or 1 lb. round steak, trimmed and cut in strips
½ cup minced onion
2 tsp. minced garlic
¼ cup butter or margarine
2 tbs. flour
2 tsps. Salt
¼ tsp. pepper
1 can (8 oz.) sliced mushrooms, drained
1 can cream of mushroom soup
½ to 1 cup beef broth
1 cup sour cream
1 tsp. parsley flakes (optional)

Brown beef in butter. Add onion and garlic. Saute until tender. Add flour, salt, pepper and mushrooms. Simmer 5 minutes. Add soup and ½ cup broth. Simmer10 minutes. Stir in sour cream and heat through. Serve with noodles. Sprinkle parsley over top.

Note: If mixture appears to be to thick, add another ½ cup beef broth.

HOME MADE SALAMI (Also good made with ground deer or elk meat)

5 lbs. lean ground beef, deer or elk
3 tsp. mustard seed
3 tsp. garlic salt
3 tbs. liquid smoke
5 tbs. canning salt or quick salt
3 tsp. coarse ground pepper

In a very large bowl, mix all ingredients very well. Kneading for at least 5 minutes. Cover and refrigerate for 3 days, mixing and kneading once a day. On the fourth day remove from refrigerator. Divide into 4 and roll into logs. Place on a drip pan over a cookie sheet. Bake at 180-200 in oven (center rack)for 9 hours. Turn rolls after 4-1/2 hours of baking. Remove and roll up in paper towels to remove excess grease. Cool and refrigerate before slicing to eat. Roll extra rolls tightly in foil and freeze up to 6 months.

Note: This is great by itself or with cheese and crackers.

BURRITOS

1 lb. ground beef
1 onion, chopped
1 bell pepper, chopped
½ tsp. pepper
½ tsp. salt
½ tsp. cayenne pepper
1 cup salsa, mild, medium or hot
1 can (15 oz.) refried beans
2 cups shredded cheddar or Mexican cheese
6 lg. flour tortillas

Brown beef and drain. Add onion, bell pepper, peppers and salt. Saute until tender. Drain again if needed. Add salsa and refried beans. Mix. Place even portions over tortillas. Sprinkle cheese over each one. Roll up, by folding ends in (halfway) continue rolling. Place seam side down in a greased baking pan. Bake at 325 for 20-25 minutes (covered) or until heated through.

MINUTE STEAKS

4 minute steaks
½ cup flour
1 tsp garlic powder
1 cup fresh mushrooms, sliced
1 can cream of mushroom soup
Salt and pepper to taste
Cooking oil

Mix flour and garlic powder. Roll steaks in flour. Use more flour if needed. Brown both sides in hot oil. Season with salt and pepper. Place in a casserole dish. Place mushrooms and soup over steaks. Cover and bake at 325 for 30 minutes or until tender.

CHICKEN

My mom raised chickens and rabbits which were for the purpose of feeding us kids. We all had to help on slaughter day. These were days I dreaded as a child. Mom would always tell us not to get attached to the animals but it was hard not to call them our pets. In order to get us to eat dinner on these nights, mom would trick us by telling my brothers and me that we were eating something else. For example on the days we put up the chickens she would tell us we were eating rabbit and the days we put up the rabbits she would tell us we were eating chicken. For the longest time I thought chicken was all dark meat. As I got older my mom shared her secret and we laughed about it. Despite these memories I still enjoy a good chicken dish. (Chicken Cordon Bleu)

BREADED CHICKEN BREASTS

4 boneless chicken breasts, pound flat
1 cup flour
Cooking oil
Creole or season salt to taste
Pepper to taste

Pound breasts just enough to flatten evenly. Coat in flour using additional flour if needed. Heat oil in lg. frying pan. Put enough oil to fry 1 side of breasts. Don't cover breasts with oil. Heat on high until sizzling. Turn heat to medium-high. Place breast in hot oil. Season to taste. Cook until golden brown. Flip over and do the same to other side. Cook until golden brown. Remove from oil.

Note: I like to put my breast (after removing from oil) back in the oven in a casserole dish, uncovered at 325 for additional 15 minutes. These are great for chicken sandwiches, eating by themselves with a side dish or dipping.

PARMESAN CHICKEN

6 chicken breasts (I prefer removing the skin)
2 cups parmesan cheese
1/8 cup parsley flakes
2 tbs. dried oregano
2 tsp. paprika
1 tsp. salt
1 tsp. pepper
1/8 tsp. garlic powder
1 cup butter or margarine, melted

In a medium bowl combine cheese, parsley, oregano, paprika, salt and pepper. Dip chicken in butter, then coat with cheese/spice mixture. Place in a greased baking pan, breast side up. Bake at 350 for 40-45 minutes or until chicken is cooked through.

CHICKEN & DUMPLINGS

1 pound fryer chicken, boiled, skinned and de-boned
2 quarts chicken broth
½ cup sliced celery
½ cups sliced carrots
1 tsp. parsley flakes
1 tsp. salt
¼ tsp. pepper

Dumplings:

¾ cup flour
1/2 tbs. flaked parsley
1 tsp. baking powder
¼ tsp salt
Dash of ground nutmeg
1/3 cup milk
1 egg, slightly beaten
1 tbs. oil

Gravy:

¼ cup flour
½ cup water
¼ tsp. salt
1/8 tsp. pepper

In a lg. saucepan or Dutch oven bring to boil, chicken, broth, celery, carrots, parsley, salt and pepper. Boil until carrots are tender. In a mixing bowl, combine dumpling ingredients of flour, parsley, baking powder, salt and nutmeg. Stir in milk, egg and oil. Drop by tbs. onto boiling broth. Cover and cook without lifting lid for 12-15 minutes or until dumplings are tender. Mix gravy ingredients in saucepan. Simmer until thickened stirring constantly. Remove dumplings and chicken with slotted spoon into serving dish. Pour gravy over top.

CHICKEN POT PIE

Pastry:
1-1/2 cups flour
1 tsp. salt
1/3 cup chilled butter cut in pcs.
1 lg. egg
2-3 tbs. ice water

Filling:
4 cups cooked chicken, cubed
1 tbs. butter
1 lb. fresh mushrooms sliced
¼ cup dry white wine or water
1-1/2 cups whipping cream
3 tbs. flour
1-1/2 tsp. paprika
½ tsp. salt
½ tsp. pepper
¾ cup chicken broth

Glaze:
1 egg, beaten

Prepare pastry in a medium bowl. Mix together flour and salt. Using a fork or pastry blender cut in butter until coarse. In a small bowl, beat egg and water. Add flour mixture until soft dough forms. Shape in a ball, wrap tightly in saran wrap and chill in refrigerator, for 1 hour.

Prepare filling by melting butter in a lg. skillet. Add mushrooms. Saute until liquid evaporates. Add wine and cook until it is almost evaporated. Add chicken and stir. Set aside. In a medium saucepan. Whisk cream, flour, paprika, salt and pepper. Cook over low heat until thickened., stirring constantly. Remove from heat. Pour sauce over chicken. Mix. Place chicken in a greased 2 quart casserole dish.

On a floured surface, roll pastry dough out to fit the top of the 2 quart casserole dish. Place pastry over chicken, trim and seal edges. Use trimmings to decorate top pastry by cutting leaves, flowers or designs. Place this on top of sealed pastry. Brush with glaze. Bake at 400 for 25-30 minutes or until crust is golden brown and filling is bubbly. Cool slightly before serving.

CHICKEN CACCIATORE

3 lbs. boneless chicken, cut in pcs.
3 tbs. oil
1 cup onions, halved and sliced thin
3 tsp. minced garlic
1 can (1lb) tomatoes, not drained
1 can (8oz) tomato sauce
1 tsp. salt
1 tsp. oregano
1 tsp. celery salt
¼ tsp. pepper
½ lb. shredded mozzarella cheese

In a lg. skillet, brown chicken in hot oil. Remove and drain chicken. Saute onions and garlic in remaining oil until tender. Add tomatoes, tomato sauce and seasonings. Boil, then simmer 25-30 minutes. Place chicken & sauce in 1-1/2 quart greased casserole dish. Cover and bake at 350 for 30 minutes. Sprinkle with cheese. Return to oven for a few minutes until cheese melts.

HAWAIIAN CHICKEN

1 whole chicken (3-4 lb) cut (legs, breasts, wings, etc.)
3/4 cup flour
½ cup bread crumbs
1 tsp. season salt
¼ tsp. pepper
1 stick butter
Cooking oil
1 can pineapple chunks (do not drain)
1 cup sugar
2 tbs. cornstarch
1 cup cider vinegar
2 chicken bouillon cubes
1 lg. bell pepper, sliced in thin strips
1 onion, halved and sliced in thin strips

Mix flour, bread crumbs, season salt and pepper. Dip chicken in flour mixture. In a lg. skillet heat butter and enough oil to cover bottom 1 inch. Brown chicken on both sides. Remove chicken to a greased roasting pan with skin sides up. In a saucepan, mix pineapple juice, sugar, cornstarch, vinegar, and bouillon cubes. Bring to a boil for 2 minutes, stirring constantly. Pour over chicken. Bake uncovered at 350 for 30 minutes. Place evenly the pineapple chunks, bell pepper and onion strips over chicken. Return to oven for 30 minutes or until chicken is tender.

ALMOND CHICKEN

1-1/2 lb. boneless chicken breasts, cut in ½ inch cubes
1 tsp. ground ginger
2 tsp. honey
1 tbs. cornstarch
3 tbs. soy sauce
12 oz. Chinese pea pods (fresh or frozen) thawed
¼ cup oil
1 cup whole almonds
3 tbs. water
1/3 cup sherry

In a bowl, mix ginger, honey, cornstarch and water. Mix until cornstarch dissolves. Add soy sauce and sherry. Mix. In a wok or skillet, heat oil. Over medium heat add almonds, stir and cook about 3 minutes. Add chicken, cook until white. Add sherry mixture. Cook until sauce thickens. Add peas. Stir fry until hot and well glazed.

LEMON-GARLIC CHICKEN

2 lb. chicken thighs, skinned
¼ cup lemon juice
2 tbs. dark karo
2 tsp. Worcestershire
4 garlic cloves, chopped
¼ tsp. salt
¼ tsp. pepper

In a lg. dish, combine lemon juice, karo, Worcestershire and garlic. Mix. Add chicken rolling in sauce and marinade covered in refrigerator for 1 hour turning chicken again in sauce after 30 minutes. Remove chicken from marinade, reserving marinade. Arrange chicken in a greased shallow baking pan. Pour reserved marinade over chicken. Salt and pepper. Bake at 425 for 20 minutes. Baste chicken with marinade. Bake 20 more minutes or until chicken is done.

CHICKEN KABOBS

4 boneless chicken breasts, cut in bit size cubes
1 lg bell pepper or sweet pepper, cut in wide strips
1 lg. onion, halved and cut in wide strips
Optional: fresh whole mushrooms
          Cubed summer squash
Teriyaki sauce

Place chicken, then pepper, then onion, etc. on skewers. Brush with teriyaki sauce on both sides. Reserve some teriyaki in small bowl for brushing while grilling. Cook on med heat grill or charcoal grill. Turning and basting until chicken is browned and done.

Note : These are also good without any of the vegetables. Place all chicken on skewers and cook the same.

CHICKEN A LA KING

1-1/2 cups cooked chicken, diced
¼ cup butter or margarine
3 tbs. flour
1 cup chicken broth
1 cup sour cream
4 oz. cream cheese
½ tsp. celery salt
½ tsp. salt
¼ tsp. pepper
1 cup frozen peas, thawed
1 jar diced pimentos, drained

Melt butter. Blend in flour, chicken broth , sour cream and cream cheese. Cook in a saucepan until thick, stirring constantly. If to thick add a small amount of milk. In a greased 1-1/2 quart casserole dish, add chicken and remaining ingredients. Cover and bake at 325 for 30 minutes. Serve over toast, biscuits or rice.

Note: Sliced mushrooms, shredded carrots, chopped green pepper, chopped onion and chopped celery may be added .

QUESADILLA

½ cup cooked cubed chicken
1-2 tsp. oil
2 flour tortillas (6 inch)
1/4 cup shredded cheddar cheese divided
1/4 cup shredded Monterey jack cheese
Salt & pepper to taste
Sour Cream & Salsa (optional)

Heat oil in a lg. frying pan. Place 1 tortilla on oil. Layer chicken and cheese, salt and pepper to taste. Place other tortilla on top. Cook in oil until bottom shell is browned. Flip (carefully) and brown other side. Remove to plate. Cut in wedges with a pizza cutter. Serve with salsa and sour cream.

CHICKEN FAJITAS

1 lb. boneless chicken, cut in strips
4 flour tortillas (8 inch)
2 tbs. cream cheese (softened)
2 tsp. oil
2 cups onion, halved and sliced thin
1 cup yellow pepper, cut in thin strips
1 cup red pepper, cut in thin strips
1 cup bell pepper, cut in thin strips
¼ cup jalapeno, cut in thin strips (2 peppers)
1/3 cup chopped fresh cilantro
¼ tsp. salt
1/8 tsp. pepper

Heat 1 tsp. oil in a wok or lg. skillet. Add onion, peppers, and jalapenos. Stir fry for 12 minutes or until crisp-tender. Remove from skillet and add cilantro, salt and pepper. Heat 1 tsp. oil in skillet over med-high heat. Saute chicken until white and done. Add pepper mix. Cook 1-2 minutes. Warm tortillas. Spread 1-1/2 tsp. cream cheese over each tortilla. Divide chicken evenly among tortillas. Roll up.

CHICKEN ENCHILADAS

1-1/2 cups boneless cooked chicken, shredded
1 cup chopped onion
1 cup shredded sharp cheddar cheese
1 cup picante sauce
3 oz. cream cheese
1 tsp. cumin
8 flour tortillas, 6 inch
1-1/2 cups taco sauce (mild, medium or hot)
Cooking spray.

Spray a lg. skillet with cooking spray. Add onion and sauté for 5-6 minutes. Add chicken, ½ cup cheddar cheese, picante sauce, cream cheese and cumin. Cook a few minutes until cheese melts. Spoon 1/3 cup chicken mixture in center of each tortilla. Roll up. Place rolled up filled tortillas in a 13 X 9 greased baking pan. Drizzle with taco sauce. Sprinkle with ½ cup cheese. Cover and bake at 350 for15-20 minutes or heated through.

CHICKEN CORDON BLEU

4 boneless chicken breasts, skin off (Beaten Flat)
4 slices of Ham, sliced thin
1 pkg. shredded Mozzarella cheese or Swiss cheese
Season salt and pepper to taste
1 cup flour
2 eggs beaten

Prepare a greased 13 X 9 shallow baking dish. Season 1 side of chicken breasts. Place 1 slice of ham over flattened (season side of) chicken. Sprinkle with about 2 tbs. cheese. Roll, folding sides in and continue rolling up. Carefully roll in egg mixture then flour. Place tightly together in baking dish with sealed side down. Salt and pepper again. Bake covered at 350 for 45 minutes to 1 hour, until brown and done. Remove cover, sprinkle with remaining cheese. Cover until cheese melts.

SWEET & SOUR CHICKEN STIR FRY

1 lb. boneless chicken, cut into 3 inch strips
1 tbs. oil
1 can (8oz) sliced water chestnuts, drained
1 cup red bell pepper, cut in thin strips
¼ cup chopped onion
2 tbs. cornstarch
2 tbs. soy sauce
1 tbs. white vinegar
1 can (8 oz) pineapple chunks, do not drain
¼ tsp. ground ginger
¼ tsp. salt
1 pkg. (6 oz) frozen pea pods
¼ cup sugar

Heat oil in wok or skillet. Cook chicken in oil until no longer pink. (5-10) minutes Add chestnuts, pepper, and onion to wok. Cook until tender, stirring constantly. Combine cornstarch, soy sauce, vinegar, pineapple with juice, ginger and salt. Mix until cornstarch dissolves. Add to vegetable mixture. Cook until sauce thickens. Stirring constantly. Add pea pods. Cook until pods and chicken are heated through. Serve over Chinese noodles or rice.

Note: 1 pkg. of frozen stir fry vegetable mix can be substituted for listed vegetables in my stir fry recipes .

SPICY CHICKEN STIR FRY

¾ lb. boneless chicken, cut into strips
3 tbs. soy sauce, divided
4 tsp. cornstarch, divided
1 tsp. minced garlic
1/8 tsp. crushed red chili pepper
2 tbs. oil
1 cup each, onion, bell or red sweet pepper, mushrooms, (sliced thin)
½ cup sliced celery
½ cup chicken broth
2 tbs. dry white wine
½ tsp sugar

Heat oil in wok or skillet. Cook chicken in oil until no longer pink. (5-10) minutes Add onion, pepper, mushrooms and celery. Stir fry for 3-4 minutes. In a bowl mix soy sauce, cornstarch, garlic, crushed pepper, wine, sugar and broth. Mix until cornstarch dissolves. Cook over vegetables until sauce thickens and chicken is done. Serve over pasta, Chinese noodles, or rice.

FIVE SPICE CHICKEN STIR FRY

1 lb. boneless chicken, cut in bite piece pcs.
6 tbs. sesame oil
1 cup carrots, sliced in very thin strips
2 cups celery, sliced thin
1-1/2 cups sliced mushrooms
¾ cup unsalted peanuts (dry roasted)
½ cup apple juice
¼ cup soy sauce
¼ cup wine
5 minced garlic cloves
½ tsp. five spice powder
½ tsp. cayenne pepper
¼ tsp. red crushed peppers
1 tsp. cornstarch

Combine ¼ cup apple juice, soy sauce, wine, garlic and five spice in medium bowl. Mix. Add chicken to marinade for 30 minutes. Heat 3 tbs. of oil in wok or skillet. Add cayenne and crushed peppers. Stir until sizzling. In oil add carrots and peanuts. Stir Fry 1 minute. Add celery. Stir Fry 1 minute. Add mushrooms. Stir Fry 1 minute. Remove from wok. Drain chicken, discarding marinade. Add 3 tbs. oil to wok. Heat till sizzling. Add chicken and cook until pink is gone. (3-5) minutes. Dissolve cornstarch in remaining ½ cup apple juice. Pour over chicken. Return vegetables to wok. Stir fry all ingredients until sauce thickens, 3-5 minutes. Serve hot with rice.

CASHEW CHICKEN

1 lb. boneless chicken, cut in bite size pcs.
1 tbs. soy sauce
1 tbs. cornstarch
1 tsp. sugar
¾ cup water
2 stalks celery, diced
2-5 tbs. oil
6 oz. cashew halves
1- (4-5) oz. sliced mushrooms, drained

Combine soy sauce, cornstarch, sugar and water and pour over chicken. Cover and refrigerate for 30 minutes. Heat 2 tbs. oil in wok or skillet. Saute cashews until golden brown. Remove cashews & set aside Add 1 tbs. oil and sauté celery and mushrooms. Remove and set aside. Add 1 tbs. oil and cook marinated chicken with the sauce. Stirring often, cook chicken until meat is white. (about 10 minutes) Add vegetables and cashews to chicken. Saute a few more minutes. Serve over rice.

CHICKEN WONTONS

3 cups cooked chicken, finely chopped
½ cup shredded carrots
¼ cup water chestnuts, chopped fine
2 tsp. cornstarch
1 tbs. water
1 tbs. soy sauce
3/4 tsp. ground ginger
1 pkg. (16 oz) wonton wrappers
2 tbs. melted butter or margarine
1 tbs. oil
Sweet & sour sauce for dipping

In a bowl, combine cooked chicken, carrots and chestnuts. In a separate bowl, combine cornstarch, water, soy sauce and ginger, Blend until smooth. Add to chicken mixture. Toss to coat. Spoon 1 tsp of chicken mixture in center of each wonton wrapper. Moisten edges with water, bringing opposite ends of the wonton together, pinching to seal. Place wontons on greased cookie sheet. Combine butter and oil. Brush over wontons. Bake at 375 for 10-12 minutes or until golden brown. Serve with sweet and sour sauce.

Note: Wonton wrappers dry out quickly so work only a few at a time, keeping others covered.

CHICKEN STRIPS

1 lb. boneless chicken strips or chicken breasts cut in strips
Season salt & pepper to taste
Favorite dipping sauce

Grease cookie sheet. Spread strips around so not to touch. Season to taste. Bake at 325 for 20 minutes. Turn over strips and season again. Cover & return to oven and bake 20 minutes or until chicken is cooked through and tender. Serve with favorite dipping sauce (Ranch, sweet & sour, honey mustard, etc)

MAKE AHEAD TURKEY

12 to 14 lb. turkey
Injecting sauce or make your own
½ stick butter or margarine
Creole, Cajun seasoning or season salt
Pepper to taste

Make Your Own Injector Sauce : Melt 1 stick butter or margarine. Mix with 1 tbs. creole, Cajun seasoning or season salt. Mix well.

Rinse turkey and remove giblets out of neck and belly. Place turkey in a greased roasting pan. With injector, inject sauce into breast, legs, etc. until sauce is gone. If you do not have an injector, cube butter, make small slits and stuff under the skin. Season the whole turkey (plentiful). Pour 1 cup water in roasting pan and seal tightly with foil. Bake as directed per pound. I usually bake between 325 and 350 for at least 4 hours. Do not peek under foil while cooking. This lets the steam out and will eventually dry the turkey out. After turkey is done, remove from oven. Drain off juices saving for gravy, stuffing broth or another day. Cool. Carefully slice turkey off with the skin and placed in a greased baking pan. After you have sliced all you can. Remove the rest of meat with your hands. Discard fat and bones. I like to layer all the white meat on one side and the dark meat on the other side of pan. Leave the legs whole for the turkey leg lovers. When all the meat has been removed and placed in the pan, pour turkey juices over the meat until covered. Cover and refrigerate until ready to re-heat and serve. Re-heat at 350 for 35-45 minutes or until hot. Just before serving drain off most of the juices.

Note: I like doing my turkey ahead of time. It allows you the time to dispose and clean up the mess. When its time to serve, it's hot, juicy and delicious. I have never had any complaints doing it this way. By keeping the juices over the meat, it stays juicy and flavorful. Usually when I am making a big holiday dinner there is so much going on with other food dishes that this makes my day easier in the kitchen. Sometimes I will also cook the mashed potatoes, stuffing and side dishes the day or night before. It allows me more time to visit and laugh with my family. It makes my big holidays meals more enjoyable to prepare. Less work, less dirty dishes and cleanup.

PORK

In February 2009, we lost a good friend of ours. James and my husband had known each other all through school and were life long friends. Cooking a pig always brought us together where many hilarious stories were shared. Everything revolved around the pig. Finding a pig, buying the pig, killing the pig, skinning the pig, cooking the pig and eating the pig. Both James and my husband were well known for their cooking skills with a pig. James could remember stories from childhood and told them like know one else could. His humor and outlook on life made you want to sit and listen for hours and the laughter lasted into the night. James loved life, his family and friends. His passing was truly a sad day for us all. We will miss him forever in our lives and his memories will never fade. Our barbeques and pig roasts will never be the same. (Smoked Boston Butt)

PORK RIB RECIPES:

3 lbs. Spareribs

Cooking Instructions: On all my rib recipes I put them on the grill over med-high heat (approx. 8-10 minutes each side) until browned or slightly singed. Remove to finish cooking in the oven. Place in lg. greased cooking pan. Mix recipe ingredients in a saucepan and simmer 20-30 minutes. Cool. Coat each side, pouring remaining or desired amount of sauce over top. Add ½ cup water to pan. Seal tight with foil or pan lid so steam does not escape. Cook in oven on medium rack at 325 for 1 hour or until ribs are tender.

SMOKEY RIBS

½ tsp. garlic salt
½ tsp. pepper
½ tsp. hot sauce
1 cup ketchup
½ cup packed brown sugar
½ cup dark karo
¼ cup brown mustard
2 tbs. Worcestershire
1 tbs. liquid smoke

TANGY RIBS

1 cup cider vinegar
½ cup ketchup
2 tbs. sugar
2 tbs. Worcestershire
1 tsp. minced garlic
1 tsp. dry mustard
1 tsp. paprika
½ tsp. salt
1/8 tsp. pepper

HAWAIIAN RIBS

1 (20 oz.) can crushed pineapple
1 cup chili sauce
½ cup packed brown sugar
¼ cup lemon juice
¼ cup white vinegar
2 tbs. Worcestershire

ORANGE STYLE RIBS

1 (6 oz.) can tomato paste
½ cup packed brown sugar
½ cup frozen orange juice concentrate, thawed (do not dilute)
3 tbs. red wine vinegar
1 tbs. prepared mustard
1 tbs. Worcestershire
½ tsp. pepper

CHINESE RIBS

½ cup hoison sauce
¼ cup honey
¼ cup soy sauce
¼ cup dry sherry
¼ cup water
2 tsp. minced garlic

CALGARY RIBS

1 sm. onion, minced
2 tbs. butter
1 cup ketchup
½ cup packed brown sugar
3 tbs. lemon juice
2 tbs. vinegar
1 tsp ground mustard
1 tsp. celery salt
1/8 tsp. cayenne pepper

MEDALLION RECIPES:

4 boneless chops (4-5 oz.) each, pounded thin or 16-20 oz. pork tenderloin
Flour, salt and pepper
Cooking oil

Cooking Instructions: Use the same instructions for each Medallion recipe. Cut pork into 2 inch pieces. Season with ¼ tsp. salt and ¼ tsp. pepper. Coat pork with flour. Heat 1 tbs. oil in lg. skillet. Saute pork in batches in oil until browned (3-4 minutes) each side. Add more oil if needed. Set aside and keep warm.

Recipes as follows:

PORK MEDALLIONS

1/2 tsp. salt
1/4 tsp. pepper
1 tbs. olive oil
1 clove garlic, minced
1 med. red onion, halved and sliced into thin strips
1 lg. sweet red pepper, cut into thin strips
1 can (13-14 oz.) chicken broth
½ cup water
1 tsp. sugar
½ tsp. dried rosemary
1 tbs. cornstarch mixed with 1 tbs. water

Add oil, garlic, onion, and pepper to the pan. Saute until tender.
Add pork to onion mixture. Mix broth water sugar, rosemary and cornstarch. Pour over browned pork mixture. Simmer until thickened.

MUSHROOM MEDALLIONS

1-1/2 cups sliced fresh mushroom
3 tbs. minced onion
¼ tsp. dried rosemary
¼ tsp. celery salt
¼ tsp. pepper
1 tsp. minced garlic
1 tbs. dry vermouth or sherry

Mix onion, rosemary, celery salt, pepper, garlic and browned pork in pan. Cook over low heat about 2 minutes. Add vermouth. Stir to blend. Spoon mushrooms over pork mixture. Simmer 3-4 minutes until heated through.

MANDARIN MEDALLIONS

¾ cup orange juice
1 tbs. cornstarch
¼ cup orange marmalade
2 tbs. lemon juice
1 tsp. prepared horseradish
¼ tsp. salt
1 can (11 oz.) mandarin oranges

½ pkg egg noodles, cooked as directed after medallions are done. Add 2 tbs. melted butter. Fold into cooked egg noodles.

In a saucepan, combine orange juice and cornstarch. Mix. Add marmalade, lemon juice, horseradish and salt. Bring to a boil. Reduce heat and simmer 2 minutes. Pour over browned pork. Simmer for 8-10 minutes. Serve over hot noodles.

MEDALLIONS IN A BRANDY-PEAR SAUCE

1 onion minced
2 tbs. butter
16 oz. sliced pears in heavy syrup
½ tsp. nutmeg
½ tsp. cinnamon
4 tbs. lemon juice
½ tsp. salt
½ cup pear brandy or pear schnapps

Saute onions and butter with browned pork. Saute for 2 minutes. Add remaining ingredients to pork mixture. Simmer for 8-10 minutes.

OVEN BAKED BBQ CHOPS

4-8 medium pork chops
1 bottle of barbeque sauce any style
Salt and pepper to taste

In a greased lg. shallow baking pan place pork chops. Brush on even layer of BBQ sauce. Flip over and brush again. Salt and pepper to taste. Cover tightly with foil. Place in oven at 350 for 30 minutes. Remove and discard of excess grease. Brush again tops of chops and return to oven at 325 for 30 minutes. Uncover, cook 10 additional minutes or until tender.

FRISCO CHOPS

4 pork chops, ½ to ¾ thick, trim fat or use boneless chops
1 tbs. oil
1 tsp. minced garlic
1 tbs. melted butter
Sauce:
2 tsp. oil
4 tbs. dry sherry or broth
4 tbs. soy sauce
2 tbs. brown sugar
¼ tsp. crushed red pepper
Salt and pepper to taste

Heat oil in skillet and brown both sides of chops. Add more oil if needed. In sm. saucepan, sauté garlic and butter. Place over chops. Combine oil, sherry, soy sauce, brown sugar, red pepper. Mix well. Pour over chops in skillet. Cover tightly. Simmer over low heat 30-35 minutes until tender. Add more water as needed. Salt and pepper to taste.

FRIED PORK CHOPS

4-6 pork chops, ½ inch thick or boneless
cooking oil
1 cup flour
Season salt and pepper to taste

Coat chops with flour (use more flour if needed). In a lg. frying pan heat oil. Use enough oil to generously cover pan but not to cover chops. Sprinkle season salt and pepper on chops (each side) while cooking. Cook on medium high until golden brown on each side. Remove chops from pan and place in greased baking pan or casserole dish. Cover and bake at 350, additional 30 minutes until tender. Uncover last 10 minutes of cooking.

CHOPS WITH SPICY PEANUT SAUCE

4-6 chops, ½ to ¾ thick remove fat or use boneless (salt & pepper to taste)
2 tbs. oil
1/3 cup milk
1/3 cup shredded coconut
¼ cup creamy peanut butter
¼ cup chicken broth
2 tbs. diced green chili peppers
1 tbs. diced pimentos
1 tbs. soy sauce
2 tsp. minced garlic
1 tsp. sugar
½ tsp. ground ginger
½ tsp. coriander (optional)

In a sm. saucepan heat milk until almost boiling. Do not scald. Remove from heat and add coconut. Let stand for 10 minutes. Strain milk, saving milk and discarding coconut. Return milk to saucepan and add remaining ingredients except oil. Cook over medium heat until thickened and smooth. Cook chops in oil (use more oil if needed) on both sides in lg. skillet for 12-15 minutes . Chops can be slightly pink in middle or cook until desired doneness. Serve chops with warm peanut sauce.

GRILLED CHOPS

8 pork chops, ½ inch thick
Creole or season salt
Pepper to taste

Season both sides of chops. Grill on medium heat or charcoal grill. Browning to almost a singe on each side. Remove to greased baking pan. Add ¼ cup water to pan. Cover tightly with foil. Bake at 325 for 30 minutes.

GRILLED HONEY GARLIC CHOPS

¼ cup lemon juice
¼ cup honey
2 tbs. soy sauce
1 tbs. dry sherry
2 tsp. minced garlic

Combine ingredients. Marinade with chops overnight. Follow grilled chop recipe.

PORK STIR FRY

2 lbs tenderloin, cubed
1/3 cup flour
3 tbs. oil
1 lg. onion sliced in thin strips
1 med. bell or sweet pepper sliced in thin strips
2 celery ribs, sliced thin
¼ cup chicken broth
1 tbs. lemon juice
1 tsp. sugar
1 tsp. ground ginger
1 tsp. minced garlic
½ tsp salt
¼ tsp. pepper
1 tbs. cornstarch
1 tbs. water
2 cups instant rice, cooked to directions

Coat pork cubes in flour. Cook in oil in lg. skillet or wok over medium heat until browned. Add more oil if needed. Discard excess oil. Combine all ingredients except cornstarch and water. Add to pork and simmer 20 minutes. Mix cornstarch and water and add to pork dish. Stir. Simmer 10 minutes. Serve over hot rice.

POLISH CASSEROLE

1 lb. Polish sausages (fully cooked) cut in ½ inch slices
2 cans cream of mushroom soup
1-1/3 cups milk
1 tbs. prepared mustard
½ cup chopped onion
2 (14 oz.) cans sauerkraut, rinsed and drained
1-1/2 cups shredded Swiss cheese
¾ cups bread crumbs (not cubed)
1 tbs. butter, melted
1 (8 oz.) pkg. uncooked egg noodles

In a very large bowl combine soup, milk, mustard and onion. Stir in sauerkraut, uncooked noodles and sausage slices. Spoon mixture in a greased 3 quart rectangular baking dish. Sprinkle with cheese. In a small bowl combine bread crumbs and butter. Sprinkle over casserole. Bake covered at 350 for 1 hour until noodles are tender.

PORK KABOBS

1 whole pork tenderloin (1-1/2 lb.)
½ cup pineapple juice
2 tbs. dry sherry (optional)
1 tbs. soy sauce
3 tbs. brown sugar
1/8 tsp. ground ginger

Combine all ingredients except pork. Set aside. Slice pork tenderloin in half lengthwise. Slice in to ¾ inch cubes. Marinade pork for 30 minutes. Thread pork on to skewers. Grill over medium heat, turning for 10-15 minutes until done. Brush with reserved marinade while cooking.

PORK FAJITAS

1 lb. pork strips
Cooking oil
1 med. onion sliced in thin strips
1 bell pepper or sweet pepper, cut in thin strips
2 tbs. cumin
1 tsp. oregano
1 tsp. cayenne
1 tsp. paprika
1 tsp. salt
4 flour tortillas, warmed (I warm them in the microwave for 30 seconds)

Place small amount of cooking oil in lg. skillet or wok. Cook pork in oil over medium-high heat, 5-10 minutes. Add onion pepper and seasonings. Toss and cook for additional 5 minutes or until tender. Serve on tortillas. Roll up & eat.

SMOKED BOSTON BUTT

1 Boston butt
Creole or Cajun seasoning
½ can beer or water
Favorite barbeque sauce

Place butt on greased heavy duty foil (or double). Make sure tin foil is large enough to wrap up butt. Season heavily, all sides, with creole. Fold ends of foil up to form a pan and pour in beer or water. Seal tight. Place on wood smoker grill using hickory wood. Cook at a temperature of 225 to 250 for 8 hours. Last hour of cooking, open to brown. Serve by itself or chopped for BBQ sandwiches. Freeze leftovers.

PORK EGG ROLLS

½ lb. boneless pork, diced
3 tbs. corn starch
2 tbs. hoison sauce
2 tbs. soy sauce
3 tbs. oil, divided
1 lg. onion, sliced in thin strips
½ lb. bean sprouts, drained or 2 cups cooked shredded cabbage
1 can (8 oz.) sliced bamboo shoots, drain & chopped
1 tbs. minced ginger root or ½ tsp. ground ginger
10 egg roll wrappers
3 cups oil

In a small bowl mix corn starch, hoisin and soy sauce. Set aside. In a wok or lg. skillet heat 2 tbs. oil over high heat. Add onion and stir fry 1 minute. Add bean sprouts and bamboo shoots. Stir Fry 2 minutes. Remove from wok. Add 1 tbs. oil in wok and heat. Add ginger. Mix and add pork. Stir fry for 2 minutes until browned. Return vegetables back to wok. Remix cornstarch mixture and stir into pork. Remove from wok. Wash and dry wok.
To fill egg rolls; spoon 1/3 cup pork mixture onto egg roll wrapper. With one point towards you fill horizontally across and just below center. Moisten edges with water. Fold bottom corner over filling and roll halfway. Fold two side corners up toward center and finish rolling. Press gently to seal.
In wok heat 3 cups oil to 375. Carefully add egg rolls, two at a time. Fry 2-3 minutes until golden brown. Drain on paper towels.

Note: If using cabbage instead of sprouts. Place shredded cabbage in microwave bowl with 1 tbs. water. Cover and cook on high in microwave 6-8 minutes, until tender.

PIZZA

1 lg. pizza crust or homemade crust Cook as directed)
1 lb. sausage, mild, medium or hot (browned and crumbled) Salt & pepper
1 onion chopped and cooked in with sausage
1 bell pepper, chopped and cooked in with sausage
1 cup chopped mushrooms
1 pkg. shredded pizza cheese blend
8 oz. pizza sauce

Evenly spread sauce over crust. Evenly spread sausage, onion, pepper mix. Evenly layer mushrooms and cheese. Bake at 375 until heated through.

SAUSAGE STROMBOLI

2 lbs. sausage, mild, medium or hot, browned, crumbled and cooled
5 cups flour
2 tbs. sugar
2 tsp. salt
2 pkg. dry yeast
1-1/2 cup warm water
½ cup warm milk
2 tbs. butter or margarine, melted
4 cups shredded mozzarella cheese
3 eggs
¼ tsp. dried basil
2 tbs. grated Parmesan cheese

In mixing bowl, combine flour, sugar, salt and yeast. Add warm water, warm milk and melted butter. Beat on low until mixed well. Turn onto a well floured surface. Knead dough until smooth and elastic. (about 6 minutes) Place in a greased bowl, turning once. Cover and let rise for 1 hour or until doubled in size. In a bowl mix cooled sausage, 2 eggs, mozzarella cheese and basil. Set aside. Punch dough down and divide in half. Roll one portion into a 15 X 10 inch rectangle. Place on same size greased cookie sheet. Spoon ½ sausage mixture lengthwise down one side of rectangle within 1 inch of ends. Fold over dough to seal by pinching edges. Cut four diagonal slits on top of Stromboli. Repeat same process for other ½ of dough and sausage mixture. Beat remaining egg and brush over Stromboli. Sprinkle with Parmesan. Cover and let rise 45 minutes or doubled in size. Bake at 375 for 20-25 minutes or until golden brown. Slice and serve warm.

SMOKED BEANS

1 pkg. dry northern or brown beans. Soak overnight and drain
2 cups cooked smoked pork or ham
½ tsp. celery salt
½ tsp. garlic powder
1 tsp. creole or season salt
Pepper to taste
Fresh baked cornbread

Place all ingredients in a crock pot. Cover with water. Cook on High until boiling begins. (2-4 hours) Turn to low for 4 hours or until beans are tender. Serve in bowl with fresh cornbread or corn pie.

Note: I like using leftover smoked Boston Butt with this recipe. Add more seasoning if needed after taste testing.

FISH – SEAFOOD

Linda was a co-worker friend of mine from Tiskilwa, Illinois. We have both moved since then and have not seen each other in many years but still stay in touch. We have some great memories together. Every year we would take a special day to Christmas shop and lunch out but we shared the same passion for fishing and gardening. She had no problems with baiting her own hook and I taught her how to filet the fish. Often on hot days we would jump in the lake to cool down and back out to fish again. Catfish were fun to catch on a full moon night. Stormy weather didn't stop us either. She was my fishing buddy and together we created some good stories to share with our families. Our ventures will leave me with ever lasting memories. (Fried Catfish)

SHRIMP'ly DELICIOUS

1 lb. thawed shrimp (deveined with tails on)

Marinade:

1 cup olive oil
4-5 tbs. Worcestershire
2 tbs. hot sauce
2 heaping tbs. minced garlic
1 full tbs. dried basil or Italian seasoning

Mix marinade ingredients together. Place shrimp and marinade in plastic bag overnight. Place marinated shrimp in a wok or lg. cooking pan. Cook over medium heat until shrimp are pink. Serve with side dish of rice and hollandaise sauce.

2 cups instant rice
1 pkg. hollandaise sauce, mixed as directed or homemade sauce

CRAB PRIMAVERA

¾ lb. imitation crab meat, flaked
1-1/2 cups frozen vegetable blend (broccoli, red pepper, onions and mushrooms)
¼ cup water
1-1/2 cups milk
1/2 cup grated Parmesan cheese
2 tbs. butter or stick margarine
1 tsp. dried basil
½ tsp. garlic powder
1-1/2 cups uncooked instant rice
Salt and pepper to taste

In a lg. saucepan, bring vegetables and water to a boil. Reduce heat and stir in milk, cheese, butter, basil, garlic powder, salt, pepper and crab. Bring back to a boil. Stir in rice. Remove from heat. Cover and let stand 5 minutes. Fluff with fork. Serve hot.

FRIED CATFISH

4 catfish fillets
Cooking oil
1-1/2 cups cornmeal
½ cup flour
3 tbs. creole or Cajun seasoning
1/2 tsp. pepper
¼ tsp. garlic powder

Preheat cooking oil in a deep fryer or heavy skillet. Add enough oil to cover fish. Combine all dry ingredients in a shallow dish. Rinse fillets, shake off. Coat fillets in cornmeal mixture. Fry fillets in hot oil for 3-4 minutes. Turn fillets for 3-4 minutes or until golden brown. Drain on paper towel lined dish.

Note: I like to soak my fillets in citrus soda pop for at least 2 hours before cooking.

BLACKENED GRILLED CATFISH

4 catfish fillets
Blackened seasoning
Creole or Cajun seasoning to taste
Salt and pepper to taste
4 tsp. stick butter or margarine
Lemon wedges (optional)

Rinse fillets and shake off excess water. Season both sides of fillets with all seasonings. Spray cooking spray on grill rack so fish does not stick. Place fish on grill over med. heat. Cook on both sides 5 minutes each side. Remove from grill on to a greased cooking pan or cookie sheet. Top each pc. with 1 tsp. butter and lemon squeezed. Place back in oven at 350 until fish is done and flakes. Serve hot.

BBQ TROUT

1 lg. pan sized trout (approx. 1 lb.)
Remove inners and head, leave skin on

1 tbs. lemon juice
2 tbs. Worcestershire
½ stick butter
Pinch of dill weed

On inside of trout spread butter and seasonings. Wrap trout in tinfoil. Place on grill. Cook on lower heat for 20-30 minutes or until cooked thoroughly.

SPRINGTIME CRAPPIE

2 lbs. crappie fillets
2 tsp. onion powder
2 tsp. garlic salt
1 tbs. creole or Cajun seasoning
Salt and pepper to taste
2 cups finely crushed butter flavored crackers
1 egg
½ cup beer or (non-alcoholic) beer
Cooking oil

Rinse and dry fillets on paper towels. Sprinkle each fillet with seasoning. Add extra seasoning to cracker crumbs. Beat the egg and beer. Pour into shallow dish. Dip fillets in egg mixture and roll in cracker crumbs until well coated. Heat oil in deep fryer or heavy pan with enough oil to cover fillets. Place fillets in hot oil (350) for 4 minutes each side or until golden brown. Remove and drain on paper towels. Serve hot.

TUNA CASSEROLE

2 cans (6-1/2 oz each) chunk style tuna in water, drained
6 oz. (3 cups) uncooked egg noodles
½ cup chopped celery
1/3 cup chopped green onions or scallions
½ cup sour cream
1 cup mozzarella cheese
1 cup shredded cheddar cheese
2 tsp. prepared mustard
½ cup mayonnaise or salad dressing
¼ tsp. salt
½ tsp. pepper
1 tsp. flaked parsley

Drain and flake Tuna. Set aside. Cook noodles according to directions. Rinse and drain using hot water. Combine noodles with the tuna, celery and onions. Blend sour cream, mustard, mayo and seasonings. Fold in to noodles. Top with cheeses. Bake at 350 for 30 minutes or until hot.

POTATOES
&
VEGETABLE SIDE DISHES

After my son's graduated and left home for the Air Force and college, we moved from Oregon to Wyanet, Illinois to work the family farm. We lived about 3 miles from town and there was only one neighboring home. As I was moving in I met my neighbors, Garda and Dick. Garda was at the door with a bottle of wine with warm welcome wishes. I instantly liked her. She was a classy, fun spirited woman. As years passed we became good friends. They had a beautiful home across the road from us and I admired her landscaping projects. An outdoors woman like myself, we were always waving to each other as she worked in her yard and me in my garden. Garda was always bringing me special gifts but there is one time I want to share with you. She had purchased me a plastic barrel to grow potatoes in. Potatoes take a lot of space in a garden and this barrel was to produce multiple potatoes by layering mulch as they grew. We were both so excited when it came time to harvest the potatoes. When we opened the barrel we were waiting for the potatoes to come pouring out as advertised. Guess what, there were maybe 4-5 potatoes. We laughed and laughed. I have never attempted to grow potatoes since. I thank her for her kindness and all her special gifts to me. (Easy Baked Potatoes)

DOUBLE STUFFED POTATOES

4 med. red potatoes
1 cup sour cream
1 cup shredded cheddar cheese
½ cup real bacon bits
1 stick margarine or butter, melted
Salt and pepper to taste

Place potatoes on microwave plate. Stab each potato, twice with sharp knife. Microwave 6 minutes. Roll over. Microwave additional 6 minutes or until potato is cooked through. Test by carefully inserting thin knife. Remove and cool. Slice in half lengthwise. Carefully spoon out potato center without disturbing the skins. Mix potato centers with sour cream, cheese, bacon bits, butter, salt, and pepper. Mix with mixer until smooth. Spoon mixture back into skins. Divide evenly. Place in greased baking pan. Bake covered at 350 for 20 minutes or until heated through.

TASTY MASHED POTATOES

8 potatoes, peeled and chunked
1 stick butter or margarine
1/8 cup milk
1 pkg. ranch dressing dip mix or ½ pkg. onion soup mix

Boil potatoes until done. Drain. Mash potatoes with remaining ingredients. I like using a mixer. Add extra milk if needed to make potatoes creamier.

EASY BAKED POTATOES

4 medium potatoes
4 tsp. butter or margarine
4 pcs. foil

Wash each potato. With a sharp knife stab each potato 3 to 4 times. Place on microwavable plate. Microwave on high for 6 minutes. Turn over and microwave again for 6 minutes. Insert knife to test if center if done. Remove potatoes and place each potato on pc. of foil. Slice open enough to insert 1 tsp. butter in each potato. Wrap with foil. Keep warm or reheat in oven until ready to serve.

SUPREME POTATOES

8-10 med. potatoes, peeled and cubed
1 can cream of chicken soup
3 cups shredded cheddar cheese, divided
1 cup sour cream
3 green onions
Salt and pepper to taste

Cover potatoes in saucepan with water. Boil until almost tender. Drain and cool. Combine soup, ½ of cheese, sour cream, onions, salt and pepper. Stir in potatoes. Place in greased 13 X 9 X 2 baking pan. Sprinkle with other ½ of cheese. Bake uncovered at 350 for 25-30 minutes or until heated through.

PARSLEY POTATOES

6 med. potatoes peeled and cubed
Note: If using red potatoes, try leaving the peel on
¼ stick of butter or margarine
2 tbs. parsley
1 tsp. garlic powder
Salt and pepper to taste

Cook potatoes until tender (still firm but tender) Drain. Place in greased casserole dish. Add remaining ingredients. Stir lightly. Bake at 325 for additional 20 minutes.

SCALLOPED POTATOES

8 med. potatoes, peeled and sliced thin
1 cup milk
1 can cheese soup
Salt and pepper to taste
Cooking oil

Fry potato slices in cooking oil in lg. frying pan. Cook till slightly brown. Pour milk, soup and seasonings. Stir in. Pour into greased casserole dish. Bake at 350 for additional 35-40 minutes, covered.

HASHBROWN CASSEROLE

1 bag frozen shredded hash browns
1 can cream of mushroom soup
1 jar real bacon bits
1 (16 oz.) sour cream
2 bags shredded cheddar cheese or 1 bag cheddar & 1 bag mozzarella
2 cups corn flakes, crumbled
4 tbs. butter or margarine

Grease 16 X 9 pan. Brown hash browns, spread in pan. Mix together sour cream, cream of mushroom, & bacon bits. Spread over hash browns. Sprinkle cheese over sour cream mixture. Mix cornflakes and melted butter. Spread cornflakes over mixture. Bake at 350 for 1 hour, covered. Uncover until golden brown. Stand for 5 minutes before serving.

GOOD OLE FRIED TATORS

8 med. potatoes, peeled, cubed
Note: If using red potatoes, try leaving the peel on
1 med. onion chopped
1 bell pepper, chopped
Creole or season salt to taste
Pepper to taste
1/8 tsp. garlic powder
½ cup cooking oil

Place oil in lg. frying pan. Heat and add potatoes and seasonings. Cook uncovered stirring occasionally.

Cook for approx. 30 minutes. After potatoes begin to brown or crisp up add onion and pepper. Cover and finish cooking until tender.

STEAK FRIES

6-8 red potatoes
Creole or season salt
Salt & Pepper to taste

Wash and cut potatoes in half, lengthwise. Slice halves into ½ in. wedges. Place on greased cookie sheet with peel side down. Spray with cooking spray. Sprinkle seasonings over potato wedges. Bake uncovered at 375 until brown. About 30-35 minutes.

Note: if you don't have cooking spray. Place potato wedges in freezer bag, coat with oil, shake and place on cookie sheet.

POTATO PATTIES

1-2 cups leftover mashed potatoes
¼ cup minced onion
1 egg, beaten
Salt and pepper to taste
Cooking oil or butter

Mix all ingredients together. Make patties and fry in sm. amount of oil or butter until both sides are golden brown.

STUFFING

1 bag seasoned bread crumbs (cubed) not crushed or 4 cups homemade crumbs
¾ to 1 lb sausage
1 medium onion, chopped
½ whole bunch celery, chopped
1 pk. Turkey gravy mixed with 1 cup water & 1 cup turkey broth or water
1 stick butter
Salt and pepper to taste

Pour breadcrumbs in lg. greased cooking dish or pan. Set aside. In a lg. skillet brown sausage, draining grease. Add 1 stick butter, onions and celery. Simmer until tender. Add to bread crumbs. Salt and pepper to taste. Add turkey liquid over crumbs and mix. Cover and bake at 350 for 3-35 minutes or until hot. Add additional broth if needed to keep from drying out.

Note: Make your own bread crumbs by laying out bread slices on a cookie sheet. Season lightly with a little sage, season salt and pepper. Slice in cubes and toast in oven till dry.

DILL POTATOES AU GRATIN

1 can cream of celery soup
½ cup sour cream
3 green onions, chopped
2 tbs. lemon juice
1 tbs. fresh dill or 1 tsp. dill weed
1 tsp. black pepper
½ tsp. grated lemon peel (optional)
3 cans sliced potatoes, drained (or) 5 med. peeled & sliced potatoes sliced and cooked down
1/3 cup shredded cheese

Preheat oven to 375. Grease a casserole dish. In bowl, combine soup, sour cream, onion, lemon juice, dill, pepper, and lemon peel. Stir in potatoes. Sprinkle with cheese. Bake 35-40 minutes or until top is golden and bubbling.

SWEET & SOUR CABBAGE

1 – 2lb. head red cabbage
3 tbs. butter or bacon drippings
1 med. red onion, chopped
1 lg. tart apple, unpeeled, cored and diced
¼ cup orange marmalade
1/3 cup cider or red wine vinegar
½ cup water, beer or red wine
1 tbs. brown sugar
1 tbs. honey
2 tbs. caraway seed
Salt and pepper to taste

Wash cabbage. Remove tough outer leaves and cut into quarters. Cut out core and cut quarters crosswise into 1/8 in. strips. Set aside. In a 4 qt. saucepan, sauté onion and apple in butter for 5 minutes. Add marmalade, vinegar, water, brown sugar, honey, salt and pepper. Bring to a boil, stir and set aside. Add cabbage. Cover and simmer, stirring occasionally, until cabbage is tender. (about 30 minutes) Add caraway seed. Serve,

CALICO BEANS (A Terrific Dish for any Barbecue)

½ lb. ground beef
½ lb. bacon, cut in 1 in. pcs.
1 onion, chopped
¾ cup catsup
1 tsp. salt
2 tsp. prepared mustard
2 tsp. vinegar
1 cup packed brown sugar
1 can pork & beans, do not drain
1 can kidney or red beans, do not drain
1 can butter or lima beans, do not drain

Cook bacon until slightly crispy. Set aside. Brown ground beef in bacon grease .
Drain excess grease. Add chopped onion and cook until onion is tender.
In a large baking dish, Mix all ingredients together. Do not drain the beans. Bake at
350 for 50-60 minutes. Stir half way through cooking

Note: If using a crock pot. Cook on high until boiling.

DEEP FRIED OKRA & MUSHROOMS

Desired amount of:
Fresh Okra (2-3 inch) or Fresh Mushrooms (small to medium in size)
Cooking oil
1 cup flour
1-2 eggs beaten
1 tbs. Creole or season salt
Salt & pepper to taste

Mix creole with flour in a small bowl. Heat 1 inch of oil in cooking pan until it
sizzles. Dip okra or mushrooms in egg, then flour and drop in oil, 4-6 at a time. Roll
over while cooking to brown on both sides. Remove when golden brown and drain
on paper towels. Salt and pepper to taste. Serve hot.

SPANISH RICE

½ lb. sliced bacon, diced (Cook to a crisp)
2 cans (28 oz each) diced tomatoes with liquid
2 cans (8 oz each) chopped green chilies
1 can tomato sauce
½ tsp. salt
¼ tsp. pepper
 2 cups instant uncooked rice

Mix rice, bacon and other ingredients in a greased wok or skillet. Bring to boil. Simmer on low-med heat for about 35- 40 minutes until rice is tender. Stir to prevent scorching.

PORK FRIED RICE

½ lb. cooked pork, shredded or ground pork, browned
1 onion, chopped
2 cloves garlic, minced
1 red or bell pepper, diced
¼ lb. mushrooms, sliced
2 tsp. oil
3 cups cooked rice
3 tbs. soy sauce
½ cup frozen peas, thawed
4 eggs, scrambled
1 pkg. fried rice seasoning mix (Mix as directed)

Saute in oil, onion, garlic, peppers and mushrooms. Add all other ingredients. Heat in a greased casserole dish at 300 for 30 minutes or heated or stir fry in wok or lg. pan until heated.

Note: When I have leftover cooked pork. I freeze it and use it for this dish.

CASHEW ASPARAGUS

1 lb. fresh asparagus, trimmed and sliced to 1 in. pieces
1-1/2 cups sliced mushrooms
1 med. onion, sliced in thin wedges
¼ cup chopped red sweet pepper
2 tbs. margarine or butter
1 tsp. cornstarch
¼ tsp. pepper
1 tbs. teriyaki sauce
1 tbs. dry sherry
3 tbs. cashew halves

Place asparagus in microwave bowl or steamer. Add a little water, Cover with plastic and microwave on high until tender. (About 8-10 minutes) Add mushrooms, onion and red pepper. Cover and steam again for additional 5 minutes or until tender. Discard liquid. In saucepan, melt margarine. Stir in cornstarch and pepper. Add teriyaki sauce, sherry and 2 tsp. water. Cook until thickened. Toss into asparagus dish. Heat through. Top with cashews.

Note: If using canned asparagus and mushrooms, drain first. It won't have to cook as long as fresh. Just heat then add other ingredients.

SPINACH MANICOTTI

1 carton (15 oz.) ricotta cheese
1 pkg. (10 oz.) frozen spinach, thawed and squeezed or 1 lg. can spinach drained and squeezed.
1-1/2 cups shredded mozzarella cheese, divided
¾ cup shredded parmesan cheese, divided
1 egg
2 tsp. parsley
½ tsp. onion powder
½ tsp. pepper
1/8 tsp. garlic powder
2 jars (28 oz. each) spaghetti sauce or homemade
1-1/2 cups water
1 pkg. (8 oz.) manicotti shells

In a lg. bowl, combine ricotta, spinach, 1 cup mozzarella, ¼ cup parmesan, egg, parsley, onion powder, pepper, and garlic powder. Set aside. In another bowl, combine spaghetti sauce and water. Spread 1 cup sauce in ungreased 13 X 9 X 2 in. baking pan. Stuff uncooked manicotti with spinach mixture. Arrange in pan over sauce. Pour remaining sauce over manicotti. Sprinkle with remaining cheeses. Cover and refrigerate for 8 hours or overnight. Remove 30 minutes before baking. Bake uncovered in preheated oven at 350 for 40-50 minutes or until heated through.

CREAMY BROCOLLI CASSEROLE

2 pkg. frozen broccoli, thawed and drained or 2 heads fresh (steamed)
1 can cream of chicken soup
2 tsp. lemon juice
½ cup crushed seasoned stuffing
1 tbs. melted margarine or butter
¼ cup shredded cheddar cheese

Note: Make your own stuffing. Cube bread slices, sprinkle some season salt and pepper. Toast bread cubes.

Place broccoli in a greased 8 in. square baking pan. Combine soup and lemon juice. Pour over broccoli. Toss stuffing and margarine. Sprinkle over soup mixture. Cover and bake at 350 for 25-30 minutes. Uncover and sprinkle with cheese. Bake a few minutes longer until cheese is melted.

CAULIFLOWER DISH

1 head of cauliflower (steamed) or 2 pkg. frozen, thawed and drained
1 can cheese soup
½ stick butter or margarine
Salt and pepper to taste

Place cauliflower in greased casserole dish. Mix soup into cauliflower. Salt and pepper. Cover and microwave until heated or bake at 350 until heated. (about 30 minutes)

GREEN BEANS

1 can green beans (any style) not drained
¼ minced onion
2 tbs. bacon bits
Salt and pepper to taste

Add all ingredients in saucepan. Simmer for 15 minutes.

Note: If using fresh garden green beans. Cook the green beans until tender. Drain. Add ingredients and enough water to cover. Simmer for 15-20 minutes.

KOOL PEPPERS

4 oz. cream cheese
¼ cup chopped jalapeno peppers
¼ cup chopped green onion
½ tsp. minced garlic
Dash of salt
6 – 7 in. flour tortillas, quartered
2 egg yolks, beaten
Serve with salsa (optional)

Mix cream cheese, peppers, onions, garlic and salt. Set aside. Quarter tortillas.
Divide mixture evenly on tortillas. Fold each tortillas pc. in to three-dimensional
triangle and seal edges with beaten yolks. Heat oil to 350, (2-3 in. standing oil). Place
2-3 triangles in hot oil. Fry for about 45 seconds or until golden brown. Drain on
paper towels. Serve immediately.

ZUCCHINI CASSEROLE

3 med. zucchini, sliced (about 6 cups)
3 tbs. oil, divided
1 med. onion
1 clove garlic, minced
1 can (28 oz.) diced tomatoes, do not drain
1 tsp. basil
½ tsp. oregano
½ tsp. garlic salt
¼ tsp. pepper
1-1/2 cups stuffing mix
Note: Make your own stuffing. Cube bread slices & toast cubes.
½ cup grated parmesan cheese
¾ cup mozzarella cheese, shredded

Ina lg. skillet, cook zucchini in 1 tbs. Oil until tender. (5-6 minutes) Drain and set
aside. In the same pan sauté onion, garlic and remaining oil for 1 minute. Add
tomatoes, basil, oregano, garlic salt and pepper. Simmer uncovered for 10 minutes.
Remove from heat and gently stir in zucchini. Place in ungreased 13 X 9 X 2 baking
pan. Top with stuffing mix and parmesan cheese. Cover and bake at 350 for 20
minutes. Uncover and sprinkle mozzarella cheese over top. Return to oven for 10
minutes or until golden brown.

TURNIPS

6-8 medium turnips peeled
4 tbs. sugar
1 tsp. crushed red peppers
Salt and pepper to taste

Cut turnips in half lengthwise. Slice each half into ¼ in. slices. Place in saucepan. Add water just to cover. Add sugar and peppers. Bring to boil. Simmer until tender.

CORN

2 cups sweet corn (cut off the cob) or 2 cans corn (drained)
2 tbs. butter or margarine
1 sm. jar pimentos (chopped & drained)
1 tsp. sugar
1/8 tsp. salt
Pepper to taste

Add all ingredients. Simmer until heated
Note: If using fresh sweet corn. Boil corn first for 3 minutes.

YELLOW SUMMER SQUASH

2-3 medium yellow squash (do not peel)
1 pint stewed tomatoes (drained)
1 medium onion sliced (thin)
1 clove garlic (crushed)
½ tsp. creole or season salt
Salt and pepper to taste
2 tbs. cooking oil

Slice squash in halve, lengthwise. Slice into thin pieces. Place cooking oil in lg. frying pan. Place all ingredients in pan. Simmer until squash is good and tender.

EGGPLANT

1 med. eggplant
2 med. tomatoes, seeded and chopped
1 sm. can diced green chili peppers, drained
½ tsp. oregano
¼ tsp. cumin
½ cup shredded Monterey jack cheese

Peel eggplant and cut crosswise into ½ in. slices. Place slices in a greased 12 X 7 X 2 microwave baking dish. Add 2 tbs. water. Cover lightly with plastic wrap. Microwave on high 5-7 minutes. Drain. Combine remaining ingredients except cheese. Pour over eggplant. Microwave again (uncovered) for 2 minutes or until heated through. Sprinkle with cheese. Let stand covered until cheese melts.

Note : I also cook this in the oven. Bake at 350 until eggplant is tender. Add remaining ingredients except cheese. Put back in oven for 15 minutes or heated through. Sprinkle cheese over top.

BREADS, ROLLS, BISCUITS, & MUFFINS

Eight years ago I married a southern gentleman from McCrory, Arkansas. I relocated to McCrory where he was born and raised. For the first 4 years we were very busy building up his business and developing a piece of property we purchased to become our home. It happened one day after we had added on to our living room that this lovely lady showed up at our house to look at a piece of furniture we had for sale. We talked for awhile and when she left, I told my husband that I wanted to know her better. It wasn't hard to forget her name since it was the same as mine, Darlene. Somehow in our busy schedules, we connected, and I was invited over to her home for coffee. I made some muffins to take along. How can you go wrong with coffee and muffins? We became the best of friends and I feel like I have known her all my life. Darlene and her husband Al, have been caring for their elderly folks for many years with some passing. They have very little time for themselves but still always make special times for their friends and family. I feel honored to have met them and to be a part of their lives. I always look forward to the phone ringing with Darlene's voice on the other end inviting me over for coffee. Since then we have enjoyed our times together for lunches, dinners, barbecues, and special sweet treats. (Strawberry Muffins)

HELPFUL HINTS:

ALWAYS PREHEAT THE OVEN

MIX DRY INGREDIENTS SEPARATE, BEFORE ADDING TO WET INGREDIENTS.

WARM WATER & MILK FOR YEAST SHOULD BE 110-115 DEGREES

EGGS SHOULD BE BEATEN BEFORE ADDING TO INGREDIENTS

SHORTENING RECIPES CAN BE SUBSTITUTED WITH OIL (BUT NOT AS GOOD).

MARGARINE CAN BE USED INSTEAD OF BUTTER (BUT NOT AS GOOD)

FLOUR USED IS ALL PURPOSE FLOUR

YEAST USED IS ACTIVE DRY YEAST

POWDERED BUTTERMILK CAN BE USED BUT FOLLOW INSTRUCTIONS

TSP. = TEASPOON

TBS. = TABLESPOON

COUNTRY WHITE BREAD

2 packages yeast
2 cups warm water
½ cup sugar
1 tablespoon salt
2 eggs, beaten
¼ cup vegetable oil
6 ½ to 7 cups flour

In large bowl, dissolve yeast in warm water
Add sugar, salt, eggs, oil and 3 cups flour
Beat until smooth
Stir in enough flour to form a soft dough
Knead on floured surface until smooth
Place in greased bowl
Cover and let rise; 1 hour or until doubled
Punch dough down
Divide in half
Place in two greased 9X5 loaf pans
Cover & let rise; 1 hour or doubled in size
Bake at 375 for 25-30 minutes
Remove from pans; let cool on wire racks

SWEET CORN BREAD

1 cup flour
1 cup cornmeal
¼ cup sugar
2 teaspoon salt
1 egg
1 cup sour cream
1/3 cup milk
¼ cup butter or margarine (softened)

In bowl combine dry ingredients
In another bowl, combine egg, sour cream,
milk and butter
Stir into dry ingredients
Pour in greased 8 inch square pan
Bake at 400 or until toothpick inserted
In center comes out clean
Serve Warm

HONEY WHEAT BREAD

1 pkg. yeast
2 ½ cups warm water
1 tsp salt
½ cup honey
1/3 cup molasses or karo
1/3 cup butter or margarine (softened)
2 – 4 cups flour
2 ½ cups whole wheat flour
1 ½ cups rye flour

Dissolve yeast in warm water in a large bowl, add salt, honey,
Molasses , margarine, 1 ½ cups flour & whole wheat flour
Blend
Stir in Rye flour & ½ to 1 cup flour until dough pulls away from bowl
Knead on floured surface using extra flour as needed
Place dough in greased bowl, cover, let rise 1 ½ -2 hours
Punch down
Divide into 2 loaves
Place in greased loaf pans
Cove, let rise in warm area until doubled in size (1 – ½ hours0
Bake at 350 for 35 – 40 minutes
Remove from pans, cool on wire racks

RYE BREAD

1 pkg. yeast
¼ cup warm water
¼ cup brown sugar
¼ cup karo or molasses
1 Tablespoon salt
2 Tablespoon melted shortening
1 ¼ hot water
2 ½ cups rye flour
3 Tablespoon caraway seeds
3 ½ cup flour

Dissolve yeast in warm water, In a large bowl combine brown sugar, karo, salt &
shortening. Add hot water until sugar dissolves. Stir in rye flour. Beat well. Add
Yeast and caraway seeds. Mix well. Add enough flour to make a soft dough. Knead.
Cover in greased bowl until doubled (1 – ½ hours). Punch down and divide in half.
Cover for 10-15 minutes. Punch down and place in two loaf pans. Cover and let rise
until double in size. Bake at 375 for 25-30 minutes. For soft crust, brush with some
butter. Remove loafs to cool on wire rack.

HOMEMADE WHITE BREAD

1 package dry yeast
1 tablespoon sugar
1 2/3 cups warm milk
2 tablespoons butter or margarine
4 ¼ cups flour plus additional
½ cup flour
1 ½ teaspoon salt
Cooking spray

Dissolve yeast and sugar in warm milk; let stand 5 minutes
Stir in butter
Add 4 ¼ cups flour and salt
Stir until blended
Knead until smooth, adding extra flour a bit at a time
Place dough in large bowl coated with cooking spray
Cover and let rise; 1 hour or until doubled in size
Punch dough down; let rise 5 minutes
Roll out into rectangle; 14X7
Roll up tightly; pinch seams and ends
Place roll, seam side down, in a 9X5 loaf pan coated
with cooking spray
Cover; Let rise 1 hour or double in size
Preheat oven to 350
Bake, uncovered , 45 minutes or until loaf is
Browned on bottom
Remove from pan; cool on wire rack

BLUE CHEESE BREAD

6 green onions, chopped (sauté with 3 tbs. butter)
2 cups flour
3 tbs. sugar
2-1/2 tsp. baking powder
1 tsp. salt
1 tsp. ground mustard
4 tbs. butter (not melted)
1 egg
1 cup evaporated milk
1 cup crumbled blue cheese
2 tbs. grated Parmesan

Mix all dry ingredients. Cut butter in until crumbly. Stir in egg and milk. Fold in onion and cheeses. Pour in a greased 4 X 8 loaf pan. Bake at 325 for 50 minutes.

ZUCCHINI BREAD

2 cups zucchini chopped in blender
1 cup oil
3 eggs
1 tsp, vanilla
2 ½ cups sugar
3 cups flour
2 tsp. cinnamon
1 tsp. salt
1 tsp. baking soda
1 ½ tsp. baking powder

Mix all ingredients. Pour in a greased and floured (2) loaf pans.
Sprinkle with 1 cup nuts , 2 tsp. sugar and 1 Tbs. cinnamon.
Bake 1 hour at 350.

APPLESAUCE BREAD   or (Pear Bread)

4 eggs
1 ½ cups sugar
1 cup oil
2 cups applesauce or (pear sauce)
2/3 cup milk
3 ½ cups flour
2 tsp. baking soda
1 tsp. nutmeg
1 cup chopped nuts
1 tsp. cinnamon

Beat eggs. Add sugar, oil, sauce, and milk. Combine remaining ingredients. Mix
well. Pour into 3 loaf pans. Bake at 350 for 1 hour or until done. Freezes well.

ENGLISH MUFFIN BREAD

5 cups of flour (divided)
2 pkgs. Yeast
1 Tbs. Sugar
2 Tsp. salt
¼ Tsp. baking soda
2 cups warm milk
½ cup warm water

Combine 2 cups flour, yeast, sugar, salt, and baking soda, in large bowl. Add warm milk and water; beat for about 3 minutes. Stir in remaining flour. Batter will be stiff. Grease 2 loaf pans. Spoon in batter. Bake 350 for 30-35 minutes or until center is done.

POPPY SEED BREAD

2 cups sugar
1 ¼ cups milk
¾ cup oil
3 eggs
2 Tbs. poppy seeds
1 ½ tsp. vanilla
1 tsp. almond extract
3 cups flour
1 ½ tsp. baking powder
½ tsp. salt

Combine all ingredients except flour, Mix well with mixer. Add flour, mix well. Pour into 2 greased and floured loaf pans. Bake at 350 for 65 minutes or until center is done. Cool in pans for 10 minutes before cooling on wire racks. Wrap and cool thoroughly before slicing.

GARLIC BREAD

Texas toast or white bread, cut crust off
Note: If you like it crispy, leave the crusts on.
Melted butter, Brush on 1 side of bread
Cut bread in half or 3 pcs.
Sprinkle with dash of garlic powder and salt
Sprinkle small amount of mozzarella cheese
Sprinkle small amount of shredded cheddar
Sprinkle dash of Italian seasoning

Bake on cookie sheet at 375 until toasted.

LIGHT ROLLS

1 cup warm water
1pkg. yeast
2 tbs. sugar
2 ¼ cups flour
1 tsp. salt
1 egg
2 tbs. shortening or butter

Dissolve yeast in water. Stir in half of the flour, sugar and salt. Beat by hand until smooth. Add egg, remaining flour and shortening. Beat again. Cover, let rise in warm place until doubled. Spoon into greased muffin pans (makes 18). Let rise again for 30 minutes. Bake at 400 for 15 minutes. While warm, brush with melted butter.

MAKE-AHEAD BUTTERHORNS (A favorite of mine)

2 pkgs. yeast
1/3 cup warm water
 9 cups flour, divided
2 cups warm milk
1 cup shortening
1 cup sugar
6 eggs
2 tsp. Salt
3-4 tbs. melted butter or margarine

In a large bowl dissolve yeast in water. Add 4 cups flour, milk, shortening, sugar, eggs and salt. Beat until smooth. Add enough flour to form soft dough. Turn on floured surface to knead. Place in greased bowl , turning once to grease top. Cover, let rise in warm place for 2-3 hours. Punch down, divide into 4 equal parts. Roll each into circle. Cut into eight pie wedges. Brush with butter. Roll from large side to point. Place rolls with tip down on cooking sheet and freeze. When frozen, place in zipper bags until needed. Thaw 5 hours or until doubled in size. Bake at 375 for 12-15 minutes or lightly browned.

BUTTER CRESCENTS

½ cup milk
½ cup butter softened
1/3 cup sugar
½ tsp. salt
1 pkg. yeast
½ cup warm water
1 lg. egg
3 ½ - 4 cups flour
Glaze: 1 lg. egg beaten

In a saucepan heat milk until bubbles appear on edges. Combine butter, sugar, and salt. Add hot milk, stir well. Cool to lukewarm. In separate bowl dissolve yeast in warm water. Let stand at least 5-10 minutes. Beat yeast mixture and egg into milk mixture. Beat in 2 cups flour at low speed. Mix enough remaining flour until dough pulls away from sides of bowl. Knead on floured surface until smooth. Place in greased bowl turning to coat. Cover with damp cloth. Let rise in warm place for an hour or until doubled. Punch down, divide in half. Roll each into circle. Cut into 6 wedges. Roll up into crescents. Place on greased cookie sheets. Cover with damp cloth and let rise 30 minutes or doubled in size. Brush with glaze. Bake at 400 for 15 minutes or golden brown.

PAN ROLLS

3 ½ to 3 ¾ cups flour
¼ cup sugar
¼ cup shortening
1 tsp. salt
1 pkg. yeast
½ cup very warm water (120 – 130)
½ cup very warm water (120-130)
1 lg. egg
Butter or margarine melted

Mix 2 cups of flour, sugar, shortening, salt and yeast in bowl. Add warm water, milk, and egg. Beat with mixer about 2 minutes. Stir in enough flour to make dough easy to handle. Turn on floured surface. Knead for about 5 minutes. Put in greased bowl and turn to coat. Cover in warm place for 1 hour or doubled. Grease 2 round pans, 9X1 ½ inches. Punch dough down. Cut dough in half. Cut each half into 24 pieces. Shape into balls. Place close together in pans. Brush with butter. Cover and let rise about 30 minutes or doubled. Bake at 400 for 12-18 minutes or until golden brown.

CLOVERLEAF ROLLS

1 pkg. yeast
3 tbs. sugar
1 ¼ cup warm milk
¼ cup butter or margarine softened
1 egg
1 tsp. salt
4 to 4 ½ cups flour
Additional melted butter

Combine yeast, sugar and milk, beat until smooth. Add butter, egg and salt, mix. Add enough flour to form a soft dough. Knead on floured surface. Place in greased bowl, roll over, cover, and let rise in warm place for 1 hour or doubled. Punch down, divide in half. Divide each half into 36 pcs. And shape into balls. Place three balls into greased muffin cups. Cover, let rise 30 minutes or doubled. Brush with butter. Bake at 375 for 15-18 minutes or lightly brown.

MOM'S BUTTERMILK BISCUITS

2 cups flour
2 tsp. baking powder
½ tsp. baking soda
½ tsp. salt
¼ cup shortening
¾ cup buttermilk (or dry buttermilk per instructions)

In a bowl, combine flour, baking powder, baking soda, and salt. Cut in shortening. Stir in buttermilk. Knead dough. Roll out to ½ inch thickness. Cut with 2-1/2 inch biscuit cutter (a soup can works good). Place on greased baking sheet. Bake at 400 for 10-15 minutes or until golden brown.

BASIC BISCUITS

2 cups flour
2 tsp. baking powder
3 tsp. sugar
½ tsp. salt
½ cup shortening
1 egg
2/3 cup milk
1 tbs. honey

In a bowl, combine flour, baking powder, sugar and salt. Cut in shortening. Combine egg, milk, and honey. Stir into flour mixture. (add extra flour if needed to form soft dough). Knead on floured surface. Roll out to ½ inch thickness. Cut with biscuit cutter. Place 1 inch apart on ungreased baking sheet. Bake at 425 for 10-12 minutes or until golden brown.

CORN PIE (REALLY GOOD)

1 cup butter (no substitutes)
1 ½ cup sugar
4 eggs
2- 4 oz. chopped green chiles
1 can creamed corn
4 cups shredded cheddar cheese
(or) 2 cups jack & 2 cups cheddar
1 cup flour
1 cup yellow cornmeal
4 teaspoons baking powder
¼ teaspoon salt

Preheat oven to 350
Cream butter sugar and eggs
Add chlies, corn and cheese
Mix well
Add remaining ingredients
Mix well
Pour into (greased and floured 8X12 pan)
Reduce heat to 300, Bake for 1 hour or
Until done in center
Note: Sometimes I cover with tinfoil the last ½ hour
of cooking time so it does not get to browned on top
Serve warm or cool; Can be heated back up in the
Microwave the next day

PECAN STICKY MUFFINS

2 cups flour
1 tbs. baking powder
1 tsp. ground cinnamon
¼ tsp. salt
2 eggs
1 cup milk
¼ cup oil
½ cup packed brown sugar
1 tsp. vanilla
TOPPING;
¼ cup melted butter
¼ cup packed brown sugar
1cup chopped pecans

In bowl, combine flour, baking powder, cinnamon and salt. In another bowl, beat eggs, milk, oil, sugar and vanilla. Stir into flour mixture. Spoon 1 tsp. butter, 1 tsp. brown sugar and 1 heaping tbs. pecans into each greased muffin pan. Top each with ¼ cup batter. Bake at 350 for 25-30 minutes (test center with toothpick). Invert pan onto pc. of tinfoil. Let stand 2 minutes, remove pan.

EGGNOG MUFFINS

3 cups flour
½ cup sugar
3 tsp. baking powder
½ tsp. salt
½ tsp. nutmeg
1 egg
1-3/4 cups eggnog
½ cup oil
½ cup raisins (optional)
½ cup chopped pecans

In bowl, combine first five ingredients. In another bowl, combine egg, eggnog, and oil. Stir into dry ingredients. Fold in raisins and nuts. Fill greased or paper lined muffin pan, 2/3 cup full. Bake at 350 for 20-25 minutes (use toothpick test).Cool for 5 minutes.

CRANBERRY MUFFINS

1 cup fresh cranberries (quartered)
8 tbs. sugar, divided
1-3/4 cup flour
2-1/2 tsp. baking powder
¼ tsp. salt
1 egg
¾ cup milk
1/3 cup oil
1 tsp. grated lemon peel (optional)
Cinnamon/sugar

Sprinkle cranberries with 2 tbs. sugar, set aside. In bowl, mix flour, baking powder, salt, and remaining sugar. In another bowl beat egg, milk and oil. Stir into dry ingredients. Fold in cranberries and lemon peel. Fill greased muffin pan 2/3 full. Sprinkle with cinnamon and sugar. Bake at 400 for 18-22 minutes. (test with toothpick) Cool for 10 minutes. Remove from pan to wire rack.

STRAWBERRY MUFFINS

3 cups flour
1 tsp. baking soda
1 tsp. salt
1 tbs. cinnamon
2 cups sugar
4 eggs, beaten
1-1/4 cups oil
2 cups strawberries
1-1/4 cup chopped pecans (optional)

Mix dry ingredients together. Mix eggs, oil, strawberries and nuts (optional) and add to dry ingredients. Mix to moisten. Spoon in muffin pans 2/3 full. Bake at 350 for 20-25 minutes.

BANANA NUT MUFFINS

½ cup butter or margarine
1 cup sugar
2 lg. eggs
2 ripe bananas, mashed
2 cups flour
1 tsp. salt
1 tsp. baking powder
½ tsp. baking soda
1 cup buttermilk
½ cup chopped pecans (or walnuts)
1 tsp. vanilla

Beat butter and sugar until fluffy. Add eggs one at a time. Beat well. Beat in bananas until smooth
 Mix together, flour, salt, baking powder and baking soda. Stir flour and buttermilk into egg mixture until moistened. Stir in nuts and vanilla. Do not over mix. Spoon into greased or paper lined muffin pan, 2/3 full. Bake at 400 for 15-18 minutes. Test with toothpick in center of muffin. Cool on wire rack.

FEATHER LIGHT MUFFINS

1/3 cup shortening
½ cup sugar
1 egg
1-1/2 cups cake flour
1 ½ tsp. baking powder
½ tsp. salt
¼ tsp nutmeg
½ cup milk
Topping:
½ cup sugar
1 tsp. cinnamon
½ cup butter melted

In a bowl, cream shortening, sugar and egg. Combine dry ingredients, add to creamed mixture and milk. Mix. Fill greased muffin tins 2/3 full. Bake at 325 for 20-25 minutes or until golden brown. Cool for 3-4 minutes. Combine topping of sugar and cinnamon in a small bowl. Roll warm muffins in melted butter then sugar mixture. Serve warm.

PIZZA CRUST

1 pkg. yeast
1 cup warm water
 2-1/2 cups flour
 2 tbs. oil (or olive oil)
½ tsp. salt
Cornmeal

Dissolve yeast in water. Stir in flour, 2 tbs. oil and salt. Beat for about 30 seconds. Cover for 20 minutes.

Grease two cookie sheets or pizza pans. Sprinkle with cornmeal. Divide dough in half. Pat each half onto cookie sheets with floured fingers. Prick dough with a fork. Bake at 375 for about 10-15 minutes or until begins to brown. Ready for your toppings.

CORN FRITTERS

1 cup flour
1 tsp. baking powder
1 tsp. sugar
½ tsp. salt (I like to use creole instead of salt)
2 eggs, beaten
½ cup milk
 1 tsp. oil
1 can drained corn
Oil for Frying

Mix flour, baking powder, sugar and salt. Combine eggs and milk. Add dry ingredients and beat. Stir in 1 tsp. oil and corn. Pour enough oil to a 2 inch depth for frying. Heat to 375. Drop a tbs. at a time into hot oil. Fry until golden brown. Drain on paper towels. Serve while hot.

JALAPENO HUSH PUPPIES

1 cup self rising cornmeal
½ cup flour
1 tbs. sugar
½ cup minced onion
1 tbs. minced jalapeno
1 cup milk
1 lg. egg
Oil for frying

Combine all ingredients, Mix well. Drop 1 tbs. spoonfuls into hot oil. Cool until golden brown on all sides. Drain on paper towels. Serve Hot.

Note: If self rising cornmeal is not available: add 2 tsp. baking powder and 1 tsp. salt to 1 cup cornmeal.

Try substituting the onion and jalapeno for whole kernel corn (drain well & pat dry) or minced tomatoes (remove all juice). What ever you decide to substitute, make sure you remove all excess liquid before adding to the hush puppy ingredients.

CAKES
&
FROSTINGS

I have loved making cakes since my baby boy's first birthdays. My first decorator cake was a snowman I made for Carl's first birthday. Then there was the rabbit cake for Alan's first birthday and it just continued on from there. My most memorable cake was the one I made called the exploding cake. It was a cake hollowed out with a balloon inside. The idea was to cut the cake with a jagged cake knife and it would explode. I guess I failed to read all the directions and did not inflate the balloon to its full capacity. When the cake was cut, the knife would just bounce back. Finally I pushed the knife hard into the cake and it just went Pssssssss and sunk in the middle. I guess the joke was on me.
(Exploding Cake)

HELPFUL HINTS FOR CAKES:

PREHEAT OVEN

FLOUR USED IS ALL PURPOSE FLOUR

SET EGGS OUT TO ROOM TEMPERATURE

GREASE AND FLOUR CAKE PANS

USE THE TOOTHPICK TEST; INSERT IN CENTER AND IF IT COMES OUT DRY, CAKE IS DONE

LET CAKES COOL FOR 10 MINUTES BEFORE REMOVING FROM PANS

LOOSEN SIDES OF CAKE WITH FLAT UTENSIL BEFORE REMOVING FROM PANS

PUT WIRE RACK ON TOP OF CAKE, INVERT AND REMOVE PAN TO FINISH COOLING

COOL THOUROUGHLY BEFORE FROSTING

HELPFUL HINTS FOR FROSTINGS:

DON'T USE SKIM MILK

USE STICK BUTTER OR MARGARINE. DO NOT USE OIL SPREADS OR TUB MARGARINES

1 tsp. = TEASPOON
1 tbs.= TABLESPOON

THE ULTIMATE CAKE

1 box yellow cake mix
2 cups sugar
1 lg. can crushed pineapple
1 (3oz) box instant vanilla pudding
1 (8 oz) carton of cool whip
1 cup chopped pecan
1 cup coconut

Bake yellow cake mix as directed. Simmer together sugar and pineapple in saucepan. When cake is done punch holes in cake with wooden spoon. Pour pineapple mixture over top. Cool Mix pudding as directed. Fold in cool whip Put over cake. Top with nuts and coconut.

CARROT CAKE

2 cups flour
2 cups sugar
½ tsp. salt
1 tsp. baking soda
2 tsp. cinnamon
3 eggs
1-1/2 cups oil
2 cups fine grated carrots
1 tsp. vanilla
1 cup drained crushed pineapple
1 cup coconut

Combine dry ingredients in bowl. Add eggs, oil, carrots, and vanilla. Beat until combined. Stir in pineapple, coconut, and ½ cup nuts. Pour into greased 13X9X2 in. pan. Bake at 350 for 50-60 minutes or until cake test done. Cool . Frost with a cream cheese frosting.

WHITE SHEET CAKE

1 cup butter or margarine
1 cup water
2 cups flour
2 cups sugar
2 eggs, beaten
½ cup sour cream
1tsp. almond extract
1 tsp. salt
1 tsp. baking soda

Bring butter and water to a boil. Stir into flour, sugar, eggs, sour cream, almond extract, salt and baking soda. Mix until smooth. Pour in a greased 15 X 10 X 1 baking pan. Bake at 375 for 20-22 minutes, until cake is golden brown or tests done.

WON'T LAST LONG CAKE

3 cups sifted flour
1 tsp. baking soda
1tsp. cinnamon
1 tsp. salt
2 cups sugar
1-1/4 cup oil
1/8 can crushed pineapple
2 cups diced bananas
3 eggs
1-1/2 tsp. vanilla

Mix all dry ingredients together. Add bananas and pineapple. Stir, do not beat. Bake at 350 in a loaf pan until toothpick comes out clean.

RASPBERRY CAKE (Raspberries can be substituted with blackberries, strawberries, or blueberries)

½ cup butter, softened
1-1/2 cups sugar
2 eggs, separated
1-3/4 cups flour
2 tsp. baking powder
¼ tsp. salt
¾ cup milk
1 tsp. vanilla

Beat butter, add sugar and beat until blended. Beat egg whites until stiff, set aside. Beat egg yolks until thick. Add to butter and sugar mixture, blend well. Mix dry ingredients. Add to mixture with milk. Beat until smooth. Add vanilla,. Fold in egg whites. Divide batter evenly among 3 greased/floured 9 in. cake pans. Bake at 450 for 10 minutes. Cool. Spread filling between layers and on top of cake.

FILLING:

1 box (10 oz.) frozen berries
1 egg white
1 cup sugar

Defrost berries, drain. Put berries in bowl. Add egg whites and sugar. Beat until mixture forms peaks.

APPLESAUCE CAKE

½ cup butter or margarine
2 cups sugar
2 eggs
 2-1/2 cups flour
1-1/2 tsp. baking soda
1 tsp. salt
1 tsp. cinnamon
½ tsp. nutmeg (optional)
¼ tsp. allspice (optional)
1-1/2 cups applesauce
½ cup raisins (optional)
½ cups nuts (walnuts or pecans)

Mix all ingredients. Bake at 350 for about 45 minutes. Use toothpick test.

SWEET POTATO CAKE

1 pkg. yellow cake mix
1 15 oz. crushed pineapple, drained
1 15 oz. canned or cooked sweet potato, mashed
1-1/3 cups water
2 tbs. oil
3 eggs
1 tsp. cinnamon
½ tsp. nutmeg
1 tsp. vanilla
Beat all ingredients at low speed until blended. Pour into 3- 9 in. round cake pans, greased and floured. Bake at 350 for 20-25 minutes, test with toothpick. Cool. Frost all layers with a cream cheese frosting.

RHUBARB CAKE

1-1/2 cups brown sugar
½ cup shortening
1 egg
2cups flour
½ tsp. salt
1 tsp. baking soda
1 cup milk
1 tsp. vanilla
2 cups finely chopped rhubarb

Mix and bake at 350 for 30-40 minutes. Do toothpick test. Cool.

TOPPING: ½ cup sugar
            ½ cup coconut
              1 tbs. cinnamon
 Mix and sprinkle over cake.

TURTLE CAKE

1 box chocolate cake mix
1 bag (14 oz.) caramels
½ cup evaporated milk
¾ cup butter
2 cups walnuts or pecans
1 cup chocolate chips

Mix cake according to directions. Pour half of mix into greased/floured 10 ½ X 14 pan. Bake 15 minutes at 350. Melt caramel in double boiler with milk and butter. Pour over partially baked cake. Top with nuts and chocolate chips. Pour remaining mix over top. Bake additional 20 minutes. Cool before frosting.

FROSTING;

1 cup sugar
6 tbs. evaporated milk
6 tbs. margarine
1 tsp. vanilla
8 lg. marshmallows
1 cup chocolate chips

Mix first 4 ingredients. Boil for 1 minute. Stir in marshmallows and choc. chips. Spread on cake.

CREAM CHEESE POUND CAKE

1-1/2 cups butter (no substitutes) (room temperature)
1 pkg. (8 oz.) cream cheese (room temperature)
2-1/3 cups sugar
6 eggs (room temperature)
3 cups flour
1 tsp. vanilla

Mix butter and cream cheese. Add sugar. Beat until fluffy. Add eggs. Beat well. Add flour. Beat until blended. Stir in vanilla. Pour in greased/floured 10 in. tube pan. Bake at 300 for 1-1/2 hours or tests done. Cool in pan for 15 minutes before removing to wire rack. Cool completely.

PINEAPPLE UPSIDE – SIDE DOWN CAKE

Fruit Layer:

1/3 cup butter
2/3 cup packed brown sugar
1 can (20 oz) pineapple slices, drained
7-8 maraschino cherries

Cake:

1-3/4 cup flour
1 tsp. baking powder
1 tsp. baking soda
¼ tsp. salt
¾ cup sugar
2 tbs. grated orange peel (optional)
1/3 cup butter (room temperature)
3 lg. eggs
1 tsp. vanilla
2/3 cup buttermilk (room temperature)
1 cup whipping cream (beat until stiff)

In a 9-10 in. baking pan, melt butter for fruit layer. Sprinkle brown sugar over butter. Stir until smooth. Place pineapple slices on top of brown sugar. Place a cherry in center of each pineapple.

In a bowl, mix flour, baking powder, baking soda, and salt. In a separate bowl, mix sugar, orange peel, and butter. Beat in eggs. Add vanilla. Add flour mixture and buttermilk. Mix until combined.

Spoon cake batter evenly over pineapple layer. Bake at 350 for 45 minutes. Do cake test. Immediately turn upside down onto heatproof plate. Leave pan on for a few minutes to allow syrup to cover cake. Serve warm.

ANGEL FOOD CAKE

1-1/2 cups powdered sugar
1 cup cake flour
12 eggs (whites only)
1-1/2 tsp. cream of tarter
1 cup sugar
 1-1/2 tsp vanilla
½ tsp. almond extract
¼ tsp. salt

Move oven rack to lowest position, Preheat to 375.

Mix powdered sugar and flour in one bowl. Set aside. In another beat egg whites and cream of tarter with mixer until foamy. Beat in sugar, 2 tbs. at a time on high speed. Add vanilla, almond extract and salt with last addition of sugar. Continue beating until stiff and a meringue forms.

Sprinkle sugar/flour mixture, ¼ cup at a time over meringue, folding in until sugar mixture disappears. Spoon batter into ungreased angel food pan (tube pan). Cut gently through batter with a spatula.

Bake 30-35 minutes or until cracks feel dry and the top springs back when touched lightly. Immediately turn pan upside down on. Cool for 2 hours before removing from pan. Loosen sides of cake with a knife.

7-UP POUND CAKE

1-1/2 cups butter
3 cups sugar
5 eggs
3tsp. lemon juice
1 tsp. butter flavoring
3 cups flour
1 cup 7-up or similar soda

Grease/flour a tube pan. Cream butter and sugar. Beat in eggs. Stir in lemon juice and butter flavoring. Gradually mix in flour and 7-up. Alternately. Pour into pan and bake at 325 for 1 hour and 10 minutes. Do the toothpick test. Let cool for 10 minutes then turn onto cake server.

BUTTERNUT CAKE   (Use Frosting of your choice)

½ cup shortening
1 cup sugar
2 eggs
1 tsp. vanilla
2 cups flour
1 tsp. baking powder
1 tsp. baking soda
½ tsp. salt
1 cup sour milk (to sour milk, place 1 tbs. white vinegar to 1 cup milk)
1 cup butternuts or walnuts

In a bowl, cream sugar and shortening until fluffy. Beat in eggs and vanilla.
Combine flour, baking powder, baking soda and salt. Add to creamed mixture with
the milk. Stir in nuts. Pour in greased 13 X 9 X 2 in. pan. Bake at 350 for 30-35
minutes. Do toothpick test. Cool on wire rack. Frost with your choice of frosting.

CUPCAKE SURPRISE (You pick the Flavor)

1 box any flavor cake mix

FILLING:

1 8 oz. pkg. cream cheese
1 egg
1/3 cup sugar
*1 cup chocolate chips (if using with chocolate or white/yellow cake mix)

Mix cake mix according to directions
Pour in muffin pan
Mix filling ingredients together. Put 1 tbs. of filling on top each cupcake batter.
Bake according to cake mix directions. Cool and frost

ALMOND STREUSEL

Streusel:

1 cup packed brown sugar
1 cup sliced almonds
¼ cup flour
3 tbs. butter or margarine
1 tsp. grated orange zest

Cake:

½ cup stick butter or margarine
½ cup sugar
3 eggs
1 tsp. grated orange zest
½ tsp. vanilla
2 cups flour
1 tsp. baking powder
1 tsp. baking soda
2/3 cup orange juice

Glaze:

½ cup confectioner's sugar
2-1/2 tsp. orange juice
Mix together until smooth

Streusel; Mix together brown sugar, nuts, and flour. Stir in butter and zest. Set aside.
Cake; In a large bowl using a mixer, beat butter and sugar until fluffy. Add eggs, beat well. Beat in zest and vanilla. Mix dry ingredients. Mix with egg mixture and orange juice. Mix well. Spoon half of batter into prepared tube pan. Sprinkle with half of streusel. Top with remaining batter and then again the streusel. Bake at 350 for 30-35 minutes. Test with toothpick. Cool in pan on wire rack. Turn cake onto serving place. Drizzle with glaze.

EXPLODING CAKE (Joke)

1 box cake mix (any flavor) mixed as directed
2 round cake pans (8-9 inch)
1 small balloon
Frosting

Bake cake according to directions. Cool completely. Cut a circle out of each cake leaving about 1-1/2 inch on edge. Remove centers. Stack cakes on top of each other. Blow up a small balloon to maximum volume. Place balloon inside cake. Place one cut out center piece and place on top of balloon. Frost as desired to appear as a normal looking cake. Have a jagged cake knife on hand to cut the cake. Cut & SURPRISE.

Note: You can fill the balloon with water. CAUTION. This makes a huge mess.

DESIGNER CAKES

Let your imagination go wild and create your own designer cake. The following are four examples:

Snowman Cake; use 2 (8-9 inch) round cakes. Lay next to each other to shape and decorate like a snowman using white frosting and coconut.

Worm Cake; use 2 round (8-9 inch) cakes stacked. Decorate with chocolate frosting (for the dirt) & gummy worms on top.

Rabbit Cake; 2 round (8-9 inch) cakes. Use one for the face. Cut the other for the ears. Frost and decorate.

Snake Cake; One 13X9 cake, Cool and cut into curvy strips. Attach strips to look like a snake, frost & decorate.

Tips:

*Use white frosting and food coloring to get a variety of colors.
*Cardboard is a great way to color and design a background/serving platter for your designer cake.
*Get the family involved in designing and creating a cake masterpiece.
*Use candy pieces, chocolate chips and colored frosting for making faces & designs.

CHEESECAKES : Note: Using egg whites rather than the whole egg will make the cheesecake whiter.

WHITE CHEESECAKE: (My Favorite)

1-1/2 cups finely crushed vanilla wafers (36-40 wafers)
½ cup coconut
1/3 cup butter melted
3 – 8 oz. cream cheese (room temperature)
½ cup sugar
2 tbs. flour
2 tbs. vanilla
2 egg whites
1 cup whipping cream (or: 2 cups cool whip)

CRUST: Stir together crushed wafers, coconut and melted butter. Press evenly into 9 in. springform pan. Bake at 375 for 10-12 minutes or until lightly brown. Cool.

FILLING: Combine cream cheese, sugar, flour, and vanilla. Beat until fluffy. Add egg whites. Beat on low speed until mixed. Stir in whipping cream. Pour into crust.

Place springform pan on a cookie sheet in oven. Bake at 375 for 40-45 minutes. Test for done. Cool 15 minutes. Loosen edges with knife. Cool additional 30 minutes. Remove sides of pan. Cover and chill for 4 hours or overnight.

Get **CREATIVE:** add bits of candy bars, choc. chips, butterscotch chips, or berries. Sprinkle small amount on batter and swirl carefully with a knife. If you choose, change the crust to a basic graham cracker crust. Top with your favorite fruits or berries.

GRAHAM CRACKER CRUST

2 cups crushed graham crackers & 1/3 cup melted butter

NO-BAKE CHEESECAKE

1 - 9 in. graham cracker crust (store bought or homemade)
2 pkg. 8 oz. cream cheese
1 cup confectioner's sugar
1 carton thawed cool whip

Beat cream cheese and sugar. Fold in cool whip. Spoon into crust. Chill. Add topping of your choice, such as cherries, blueberries, etc.

NEW YORK CHEESECAKE

Crust:
1-2/3 cups graham cracker crumbs (about 12)
2 tbs. sugar
2 tbs. light brown sugar
¼ tsp. cinnamon
3 tbs. butter melted

Mix and press into 9 in. springform pan.

Filling:
2 lbs. cream cheese
1 cup sugar
¼ cup flour
¼ cup heavy cream
4 eggs (room temperature)
1 tsp. vanilla
½ tsp. grated orange rind
½ tsp. grated lemon rind
¼ tsp. salt

Mix all ingredients. Spoon into crust. Bake at 325 for 1 ¾ hours. Test for done. Cool completely before removing side of pan. Loosen edges with a knife. Chill for 4 hours or overnight. Your choice for toppings or try this New York style topping:

Topping:
1 cup sour cream
2 tbs. sugar
½ tsp. vanilla
Whip until creamy

FUDGE FROSTING

½ cup sugar
¼ cup baking cocoa
¼ cup milk
2 tbs. stick butter or margarine
1 tbs. light corn syrup
Dash of salt
½ to ¾ cup powdered sugar
½ tsp. vanilla

Mix sugar and cocoa in 2 quart saucepan. Stir in milk, margarine, corn syrup and salt. Heat to boiling, stir frequently. Boil 3 minutes, stirring occasionally, cool. Beat in powdered sugar and vanilla until smooth.

SOUR CREAM FROSTING

1/3 cup stick butter or margarine, softened
3 cups powdered sugar
½ cup sour cream
2 tsp. vanilla

Mix margarine and powdered sugar until blended. Stir in sour cream and vanilla. Beat until smooth.

DECORATORS ICING

1 box (1 pound) confectioners sugar
3 egg whites
½ tsp. cream of tarter

Beat together sugar, egg whites, and cream of tarter in a bowl on low until blended. Beat at high speed, until smooth. Let sit for 7 minutes. Keep unused icing covered with a damp cloth.

BASIC BUTTER FROSTING

1/3 cup stick butter or margarine, softened
3 cups confectioner's sugar
Dash of salt
¼ cup milk
1 ½ tsp. vanilla

Mix butter, sugar, salt, milk, and vanilla. Whip until fluffy. If necessary, add a little more sugar and milk to give desired consistency.

CREAM CHEESE FROSTING

2 – (3 oz.) pkgs. Soft cream cheese (room temperature)
4 tsp. milk
Dash of salt
1-1/2 tsp. vanilla
1lb. confectioner's sugar

Combine cheese and milk in bowl. Beat until blended. Add salt, vanilla, and sugar. Beat until fluffy.

FLUFFY FROSTING

2 egg whites
1- ½ cups sugar
1-1/2 tsp. light corn syrup
1/3 cup cold water
1/8 tsp. salt
1 tsp. vanilla

Combine all ingredients except vanilla in top of double boiler. Mix until blended. Cook over boiling water, beating constantly until mixture forms peaks when beater is raised. (about 7 minutes) Remove from heat. Add vanilla and whip until desired consistency.

PIES

Taking 4-H as a young girl I learned to make a pretty awesome pumpkin pie. My mom told me that I made the best crusts so I became the pie maker for the household. My step-grandpa loved my pumpkin pies, also. Grandma passed away with cancer in her forties leaving grandpa very lonely. Having a 10 month old son, grandpa liked to come over and play with his great grandson, Carl. When I knew he was coming I would make sure I had pie and coffee. My grandpa passed shortly after. He was a kind and gentle man. As a little girl he would play all kinds of games with me, Sugar Land, Tinker Toys and Lincoln Logs were among my favorites. He would sit back with his dog "Goldie" on his lap, smoking his pipe, watching my every move. I will never forget my grandpa. (Pumpkin Pie)

CRUSTS:

One-Crust Pie
1/3 cup plus 1 tbs. shortening
1 cup flour
¼ teaspoon salt
2-3 tbs. cold water

Two-Crust Pie
2/3 plus 2 tbs. shortening
2 cups flour
1 tsp. salt
4-5 tbs. cold water

Cut shortening into flour and salt. Use pastry blender or fork. Sprinkle with cold water, 1 tbs. at a time, tossing with a fork until all flour is moistened and pastry almost cleans side of bowl. (1-2 tsp. water can be added if necessary)

Roll pastry into a ball. Do not over handle. Shape into flattened round on floured surface. For 2-crust, divide in half.

Roll pastry out in a circle, 2 in. larger than upside down pie pan. Fold pastry into fourths. Place in pie pan and unfold. Press firmly against sides and bottom.

HELPFUL HINTS:

Do not over mix or handle. Dough will tend to dry and crumble.

Flour = all purpose flour

Shortening can be substituted with lard

For a two crust pie use a floured fork to crimp two crusts together. Slide a knife around edge of pie pan to get rid of uneven edges if pie crust.

Use some narrow pcs. of tinfoil to wrap around edges of crust so the edges don't burn or get over cooked.

Place on a cookie sheet in the oven in case of bubbling over

Prick top pie crust with fork (8-10) times

If recipe calls for a cooked shell, bake at 425 for 12 minutes

All ovens bake differently. To prevent top of pie from browning to quickly, place a piece of foil (loosely) over pie for first half of cooking time.

MERINGUE

3 egg whites
Dash of salt
1 cup (1/2 jar) marshmallow crème

Beat egg whites and salt until a peak forms. Gradually add crème, beating until stiff peak forms. Spread over pie filling, sealing to the edge of crust. Bake at 350 for 12-15 minutes or until lightly brown. Cool

APPLE PIE or PEACH PIE

Pastry for 2-crust pie
1/3 to 2/3 cup sugar
¼ cup flour
½ tsp. cinnamon
½ tsp. nutmeg (optional)
Dash of salt
8 cups thinly sliced peeled tart apples (about 8 apples or peaches)
2 tbs. stick butter or margarine

Preheat oven to 425. Prepare pastry

Mix sugar, flour, cinnamon, nutmeg and salt in large bowl. Stir in apples or peaches. Turn into pastry lined pan. Dot with butter. Cover with top pastry. Prick with fork and crimp edges. Cover edges with tinfoil to prevent over browning. Remove foil last 15 minutes of baking. Bake 40-50 minutes or until crust is brown and juice begins to bubble through slits in crust. Cool on wire rack. Serve warm or cold.

CRANBERRY-APPLE PIE

Use same recipe for Apple Pie. Substitute 3 cups of apples for 2 cups of fresh cranberries. Increase sugar to 1-1/3 cups sugar and omit cinnamon and nutmeg.

PECAN PIE

3 eggs
1 cup sugar
1 cup light or dark corn syrup
2 tbs. butter or margarine melted
1 tsp. vanilla
1-1/2 cups pecans
1 unbaked pie crust

Preheat oven to 350. Prepare pie crust.

In a medium bowl beat eggs slightly. Add sugar, corn syrup, butter and vanilla. Stir until blended. Stir in pecans. Pour into pie crust. Bake 50-55 minutes or until knife inserted halfway comes out clean. Cool Completely

PEANUT BUTTER PIE

1 graham cracker crust
8 oz. cream cheese
1 cup powdered sugar
½ cup peanut butter (smooth or crunchy)
2 tbs. milk
Small carton of whipped topping

Beat cream cheese and powdered sugar until fluffy. Blend in peanut butter and milk. Fold in whipped topping. Pour in crust. Chill.

PEANUT PIE

1 baked pie crust
1 cup chunky peanut butter
¾ cup powdered sugar
3 oz. pkg. instant chocolate pudding
2 cups milk
8 oz. cool whip

Cream peanut butter and sugar together. Spread in baked pie crust. Mix pudding and milk. Spread on peanut butter layer. After pudding sets up, spread cool whip on top. Chill.

COCONUT PIE

1 unbaked pie shell
1-1/2 cups milk
1 cup sugar
¾ cup shredded coconut (make sure it's fresh)
2 eggs beaten
3 tbs. flour
1 tbs. butter or margarine melted
¼ tsp. vanilla

Preheat oven to 350 and prepare pie crust.

In a large bowl, mix milk, sugar, coconut, eggs, flour, butter, and vanilla. Pour into pie crust. Bake for 50 minutes or until knife inserted near center comes out clean. Cool to room temperature. Chill.

Note: A meringue or a cool whip topping goes will with this pie.

CARAMEL PIE

Crust:
1-1/2 cups crushed gingersnaps (about 30)
¼ cup butter or margarine melted

Filling:
¼ cup cold water
1 envelope unflavored gelatin
28 caramels
1 cup milk
Dash of salt
½ cup chopped pecans
1 tsp. vanilla
1 cup whipping cream, whipped
Optional: Caramel ice cream topping & additional pecans

Combine cookie crumbs and butter. Press into bottom of greased pie pan. Cover and chill.
Place cold water in heavy saucepan, sprinkle with gelatin. Let stand for 1 minute. Add caramels, milk and salt. Cook and stir over low heat until gelatin is dissolved and caramels are melted. Refrigerate for 1-2 hours or until mixture mounds when stirred. Stir in pecans and vanilla. Fold in whipped cream. Pour into crust. Refrigerate 6 hours or overnight. Optional: Garnish with ice cream topping and pecans.

PUMPKIN PIE

1 can (15 oz) pumpkin
¾ cup sugar
½ tsp. salt
1 tsp. ground cinnamon
½ tsp. ground ginger
¼ tsp. ground cloves
2 lg. eggs
1 can (12 oz) evaporated milk
1 unbaked 9 inch pie crust

Beat eggs in large bowl, Add remaining ingredients and mix well. Pour in unbaked pie crust. Bake at 425 for 15 minutes. Reduce heat to 350 for 40-50 minutes or until knife inserted in center comes out clean.

PUMPKIN PUDDING PIE

1 can (15 oz) pumpkin
¾ cup sugar
½ tsp. cinnamon
1 box instant vanilla pudding
1 (3 oz) package cream cheese, softened
1 carton whipped topping
1 ready graham cracker pie crust

Mix pumpkin, sugar, cinnamon, pudding and cream cheese until smooth. Spoon in pie shell. Chill until set. Top with whipped topping.

CHOCOLATE CREAM PIE

1 baked pie crust
1-1/2 cups sugar
1/3 cup flour
3 tbs. baking cocoa
½ tsp. salt
1-1/2 cup water
1 can (12 oz.) evaporated milk
6 egg yolks beaten
½ cup butter or margarine
1 tsp. vanilla
Whipped topping

In a lg. saucepan, combine first six ingredients until smooth. Cook and stir over medium heat until thick and bubbly. (about 2 minutes) Reduce heat. Cook and stir 2 minutes longer. Remove from heat. Stir 1 cup hot mixture into egg yolks. Return all ingredients back into pan and bring to gentle boil, stirring constantly so not to burn. Remove from heat and stir in butter and vanilla. Cool slightly. Pour warm filling into pie crust. Chill . Top with whipped topping before serving.

BERRY CRUMB PIE

Crumb crust & topping
1 cup almonds
2 cups flour
½ cup sugar
¾ cup butter cut in small pcs.
Filling
½ cup sugar
1-1/2 tbs. cornstarch
2 pints fresh berries (blueberries, raspberries, blackberries, or strawberries) (or)
Mix them up for Bumble Berry pie.

Preheat oven to 450
Roast nuts until toasted, Finely grind nuts in food processor. (don't over grind to a powder) In a lg. bowl mix nuts, flour and sugar. Cut butter into flour mixture until coarse crumbs form. Press half of crumb crust into bottom and sides of 8-9 inch pan or tart pan.

In a bowl, mix sugar and cornstarch. Gently fold in berries. Spoon berry mixture into crust. Spread evenly. Sprinkle remaining crumb mixture over filling. Bake until top is golden and filling is bubbly. (about 30 minutes) Cool on wire rack. Cool for 10 minutes.

COOKIES
CANDY
TREATS

This past Christmas a new family tradition was started. A family cook off. My oldest son Carl and my granddaughter Kayla (age 8) were on one team and my granddaughter Alex (age 12) and I were the other team. My youngest son Alan, the wives, (Jennifer and Bobbie), and my husband were the judges. Alex devised a dessert recipe that was worthy of being served in a five star restaurant. It was the overall winning dish in our 2008 cook off. I cannot begin to explain the pride and joy I had in her and all her enthusiasm and participation. Thinking I had an influence devolving her creative cooking ambitions will always bring a smile to my face. We had some tough competition and only won by a few points. A traveling trophy was presented and I have no doubt we will be challenged at the next family get together. I am confident that the memories created that day in the kitchen will be something we will cherish forever. (Granola Parfaits)

COOKIES – CANDY – TREATS

Helpful Hints:

Preheat oven when needed

Flour = All purpose flour

Tsp = teaspoon
Tbs = tablespoon

Use stick butter and margarine (Do not use spreads unless specified)

For candy recipes: Vanilla Extract is best instead of imitation vanilla

When cooking over a flame and not a double boiler, always stir constantly to prevent burning.

SUGAR COOKIES

2 sticks butter or margarine
1 cup sugar
1 cup powdered sugar
2 eggs
1 cup shortening
2 tsp. vanilla

Cream together

Add:
4-1/2 cups flour
1 tsp. salt
1 tsp. cream of tarter
1 tsp. baking soda

Mix all together and refrigerate until chilled. Drop by tsp. or make small balls and place on greased cookie sheet. Use floured fork to press down. Bake at 350 for about ten minutes.

WHITE CHOCOLATE MACADAMIA NUT COOKIES

½ cup softened butter
¾ firmly packed brown sugar
2 tbs. sugar
1 lg. egg
1-1/2 tsp. vanilla
2 cups flour
¾ tsp. baking soda
½ tsp. baking powder
1/8 tsp. salt
1 cup white chocolate morsels
1 – 7oz. jar macadamia nuts, coarsely chopped

Beat butter, sugars, egg and vanilla until fluffy. Combine flour, soda, powder, and salt.. Mix both mixtures together, mix well. Stir in morsels and nuts. Drop by tsp. on greased cookie sheet. Bake at 350 for 8-10 minutes.

PECAN SNOWBALL COOKIES

1 cup butter shortening
¾ cup powdered sugar
2 tbs. milk
1-1/2 tsp. vanilla

Cream these together
Add:

1-3/4 cup flour
1 cup quaker oats
½ cup chopped pecans
¼ tsp salt

Shape into round tsp. balls. Bake at 325 on ungreased cookie sheet for 15-18 minutes. Roll in powdered sugar. Cool. Reroll.

DIPPED GINGERSNAPS

2 cups sugar + additional sugar to roll dough in
1-1/2 cups oil
2 eggs
½ cup molasses or dark karo
4 cups flour
4 tsp. baking soda
1 tbs. ginger
2 tsp. cinnamon
1 tsp. salt
2 pkgs. (12 oz) vanilla baking chips
¼ cup shortening

Mix sugar, oil, and eggs. Stir in molasses. Combine dry ingredients. Mix with creamed mixture. Mix well. Shape into ¾ in. balls and roll in additional sugar. Place 2 in. apart on an ungreased cookie sheet. Bake at 350 for 10-12 minutes. Remove to wire racks to cool. Melt chips and shortening in sm. Sauce pan over low heat until melted. Dip cookies halfway in chocolate. Shake off excess. Place on waxed paper to cool.

OATMEAL CRÈME FILLED COOKIES

1-1/2 cups shortening
2-2/3 cups packed brown sugar
4 eggs
2 tsp. vanilla
2-1/4 cups flour
2 tsp. cinnamon
1-1/2 tsp. baking soda
1 tsp. salt
½ tsp. nutmeg (optional)
4 cups old fashioned oats

Filling:

¾ cup shortening
3 cups confectioner's sugar
1 jar (7oz.) marshmallow crème
1-3 tbs. milk

Cream together shortening, brown sugar, eggs (1 at a time). Beat in vanilla. Combine flour, cinnamon, baking soda, salt, and nutmeg. Add to creamed mixture. Mix well. Stir in oats. Drop by rounded tsp. on greased cookie sheet. Bake at 350 for 10-12 minutes or until golden brown. Remove to wire racks to cool.

Filling: Cream shortening, sugar, and marshmallow crème. Add just enough milk to make a spreading consistency. Spread filling on bottom of ½ of the cookies. Top with remaining cookies.

RICE KRISPIE TREATS

¼ cup margarine or butter
1 pkg. (10 oz) marshmallows or 4 cups mini marshmallows
6 cups rice krispie cereal

Melt margarine in lg. saucepan over low heat. Add marshmallows and stir until completely melted. Remove from heat. Add rice krispies. Stir until well coated. Using a buttered spatula or waxed paper, press mixture evenly into buttered 13X9X2 in pan. Cool. Cut into squares.

COOLWHIP COOKIES

1 pkg. lemon cake mix (use any flavor cake mix of your liking)
2 cups cool whip
1 lg. egg
Powdered sugar

Mix all ingredients except powdered sugar. Roll a rounded tsp. full of dough in powdered sugar. Slide on to greased cookie sheet. Bake a 350 for 7-8 minutes.

DIVINITY

4 cups sugar
1 cup light corn syrup
1 cup water
¼ tsp. salt
3 egg whites (room temperature)
1 cup chopped walnuts
1 tsp. vanilla

Mix sugar, syrup, water, and salt in heavy saucepan. Cook and stir over medium heat until mixture starts to boil. Continue cooking until a soft ball forms when tested in cold water. (drop a droplet in cold water to see if a ball forms) Beat egg whites until stiff. Pour ½ cup syrup over whites, beating fast all the time. Continue cooking remaining syrup while beating egg whites, until syrup reaches a light crack stage when dropped in cold water (this will happen quickly). Pour remaining syrup over egg white mixture, beating fast all the time. Continue beating until candy begins to hold its shape. Stir in vanilla and nuts. Drop by tsp. onto waxed paper. Cool

Note: Divinity can be tricky to make. Make sure your mixture gets hot enough to pass the cold water test but don't let it burn. It's almost easier making with a second person to help.

PEANUT BUTTER FUDGE

2 cups sugar
½ cup milk
1-1/3 cups peanut butter
1 jar (7 oz.) marshmallow crème

In a saucepan, bring sugar and milk to a boil for 3 minutes. Stir constantly so not to burn. Add peanut butter and crème. Mix well. Pour quickly into a buttered 8 in. square pan. Chill until set. Cut in squares.

EASY FUDGE

1 8 oz. pkg. chocolate chips
1 – 14 oz. can condensed milk
1 block unsweetened chocolate
1 cup chopped walnuts (optional)

Combine all ingredients except nuts in a double boiler. Heat until melted. Add nuts. Pour in a buttered 8 in. square pan. Let stand for 1 hour, then refrigerate for additional hour. Cut in squares.

PEANUT BUTTER CUPS

1 cup peanut butter
2 cups powdered sugar
¼ cup butter softened
12 oz. semi sweet chocolate chips
3 tbs. shortening

Beat first 3 ingredients at a low speed until well blended. Divide into 3. Make each into a roll and wrap in waxed paper. Refrigerate for 30 minutes. Cut each roll into ½ in. slices. Place each slice in a paper lined muffin pan. Melt chocolate and shortening in double boiler until melted and blended. Do not boil. Spoon 1 tsp. chocolate mixture over each peanut butter slice. Refrigerate until chocolate is set up. Store in refrigerator.

FUDGE BROWNIES

1-1/3 cups flour
2 cups sugar
¾ cup baking cocoa
1 tsp. baking powder
½ tsp. salt
2/3 cup oil
4 eggs, beaten
2 tsp. vanilla

Combine first 5 ingredients. In another bowl mix oil, eggs, and vanilla. Add to dry ingredients. Do not over mix. Spread in a 13 X 9 X 2 in. baking pan. Bake at 350 for 20-25 minutes or until a toothpick inserted in center comes out clean.

Note: If you like nuts in your brownies, add ½ cup chopped nuts of your choice to batter. Top with additional 1 cup chopped nuts before baking.

DISAPPEARING BROWNIES

1 cup butterscotch chips
½ cup margarine or butter
1-½ cup flour
2/3 cup packed brown sugar
2 tsp. baking powder
½ tsp. salt
1 tsp. vanilla
2 eggs
2 cups mini marshmallows
2 cups chocolate chips (12 oz.)
½ cup chopped walnuts or pecans

Melt butterscotch chips and margarine in saucepan. Set aside. Mix flour, brown sugar, baking powder, salt, vanilla and eggs. Mix in butterscotch mixture. Fold in marshmallows, chocolate chips and nuts. Spread in 2 greased 9 in. square pans. Bake at 350 for 20-30 minutes. Do not over bake. Center will appear to be soft but will firm when it cools.

APPLE NUT BARS (Moist & Yummy)

1 ¾ cups sugar
3 eggs (beat well)
¾ cup oil
2 cups flour
1 tsp. baking soda
1 tsp. cinnamon
1 tsp. salt
1 tsp. vanilla
2 cups chopped (Pre-cooked) apples
(I cook my apples in the microwave)
½ cup butterscotch chips
½ cup nuts (walnuts or pecans)

Mix all ingredients except apples. Fold in apples. Spread in greased 13X9 pan.
Spread chips and nuts on top. Bake at 350 for 40 minutes. Watch time. It can be done as early as
30 minutes depending on oven.

GRANOLA PARFAITS (Won in the Git R Done 2008 Family Cook off)

4-6 cups granola cereal (without raisins)
1 lg carton vanilla yogurt
2 bananas
Sm. bunch green seedless grapes (sliced in half)
Sm. container of strawberries (sliced)
Slivered almonds (optional)
Honey

Place small amounts of yogurt into bottom of 8 serving glasses.
Place layer of fruits on yogurt.
Place small amounts of granola & almonds on top of fruits.
Drizzle small amount of honey on granola.
Repeat layers

TURTLE CARAMELS

½ cups pecans, coarsely chopped
1 cup (6 oz.) semisweet chocolate chips
2 sticks butter or margarine
¼ cup water
1 box (16 oz.) light brown sugar
1 cup light corn syrup
1 can (14 oz) sweetened condensed milk
2 tsp. vanilla

Line a 13X9X2 in. baking pan with tinfoil. Grease foil. Scatter pecans and choc. chips over bottom of pan. Melt butter in a saucepan. Stir in water, brown sugar, and corn syrup. Bring to boil over medium heat. Stir often. Do not burn. Stir in milk and return to boil. Keep stirring. Boil 30 minutes or until candy thermometer reaches 25-266 F. (or test by dropping a small amount in ice water. If it forms a hard ball, it's ready) Remove from heat and stir in vanilla. Pour evenly over nuts and chips. Cool completely. Invert pan on a cutting board. Peel off foil and cut candy into 1 in. squares. Store with waxed paper between layers.

CARAMEL NUT CANDY

28 caramels
¼ cup butter or margarine
2 tbs. half and half cream
1-1/2 cup confectioner's sugar
1 cup salted peanuts
2 cups mini marshmallows
1-2 cups flaked coconut

Place caramels, butter and cream in a microwave dish. Microwave uncovered for 2 minutes. Stir. Microwave additional 1-3 minutes, stirring every minute until smooth. Stir in sugar until smooth. Add peanuts. Fold in marshmallows. Set aside. Sprinkle coconut in a 10 X 5 in. strip on 2 sheets of waxed paper. Using the wax paper, coat the caramel with the coconut and roll into 2 10 in. logs. Discard wax paper. Wrap logs in plastic wrap and chill for at least 4 hours. Cut logs in ½ in. slices or slice as you want to eat them.

SALTED PEANUT CHEWS

1 box yellow cake mix
1/3 cup butter or margarine, softened
1 egg
3 cups mini marshmallows

Topping:

2/3 cup corn syrup
¼ cup margarine
2 tsp. vanilla
1- 10 oz. pkg. peanut butter chips
2 cups rice crisp cereal
2 cups salted peanuts

In a lg. bowl combine cake mix, 1/3 cup margarine, and egg. Mix on low until
crumbly. Press into bottom of an ungreased 13 X 9 pan. Bake at 350 for 12-18
minutes or until light brown. Remove from oven and sprinkle with marshmallows.
Return to oven and bake for 1-2 minutes until marshmallows puff out. Cool. In a
large saucepan, combine corn syrup, margarine, vanilla and chips. Heat until chips
are melted and smooth. Stir constantly. Remove from heat and stir in cereal and
peanuts. Spoon this mixture over marshmallow mixture. Spread to cover.
Refrigerate until firm. Cut into bars.

POPCORN BALLS

2 cups sugar
2/3 cup water
2/3 cup karo syrup
1-1/2 tsp. salt
¼ pound butter
Food coloring (optional)
Pop lg. bowl or 2 bags microwave popcorn

Boil ingredients until soft ball stage. Add food coloring of your choice. Add vanilla.
Pour syrup over popcorn. Make sure your hands are well buttered. Form popcorn
balls. Cool. Wrap in waxed paper to store.

PEPPERMINT PATTIES

1 box (1 lb.) confectioners sugar
3 tbs. butter or margarine, softened
2-3 tsp. peppermint extract
½ tsp. vanilla
¼ cup evaporated milk
2 cups (12 oz) semisweet chocolate chips
2 tbs. shortening

In bowl, combine first 4 ingredients. Add milk and mix well. Roll into 1 in. balls and place on waxed paper lined cookie sheet. Chill for 20 minutes. Flatten with a glass to ¼ in. circle. Chill for 30 minutes. In a double boiler or microwave safe bowl, melt chocolate chips and shortening. Dip patties by placing each pc. on a fork. Tap off excess chocolate. Place on waxed paper to harden. Store with wax paper lining between layers.

ORANGE TAFFY

2 cups sugar
2 cups light corn syrup
1 can (6 oz.) frozen orange juice concentrate (do not dilute)
Pinch of salt
1 cup light cream
½ cup butter or margarine

In a heavy saucepan, combine first 4 ingredients. Cook and stir over medium heat until sugar is dissolved. Bring to a rapid boil, to firm ball stage or candy thermometer reads 245. Add cream and butter. Heat and stir until it reaches 245 again. Pour into greased 15 X 10 X 1 in. pan. Cool. When cool enough to handle, roll into1-1/2 in. logs or 1 in balls. Wrap individually in waxed paper. Twist ends.

BUTTERSCOTCH HAYSTACKS

1 bag of butterscotch baking chips
1 cup peanuts (optional)
10 oz. chow mein noodles
1 tsp. margarine

Pour noodles and nuts in a large bowl. Line a large cookie sheet with waxed paper. Melt margarine and baking chips in double broiler until melted. Pour over noodles and mix. Working fast place tbs. clumps on cookie sheet. Chill until hardened.

CREAM PUFF DESSERT (A favorite of mine)

1 cup water
½ cup butter (no substitute)
1 cup flour
4 eggs

Filling:

1 pkg. (8 oz.) cream cheese, softened
3-1/2 cups cold milk (not skim milk)
2 pkgs. Instant chocolate pudding

Topping:

1 carton (8 oz.) whipped topping, thawed
¼ cup chocolate ice cream topping
¼ cup caramel ice cream topping
1/3 cup slivered almonds

In a saucepan bring water and butter to a boil. Add flour all at once. Stir until a smooth ball forms. Remove from heat and let stand for 5 minutes. Beat in eggs, one at a time. Beat until smooth. Spread in greased 13 X 9 X2 in. pan. Bake at 400 for 30-35 minutes or until puffy and golden brown. Cool on wire rack. In a mixing bowl, beat cream cheese, milk and pudding mix until blended. Spread over puff pastry. Refrigerate 20 minutes. Spread with whipped topping. Drizzle over chocolate and caramel toppings. Sprinkle almonds.

HONEY BUBBLE RING

½ cup honey
1/3 cup sugar
¼ cup chopped pecans
1 tbs. orange juice
1 tsp. cinnamon
½ tsp. grated orange peel
3 tubes refrigerated (12 0z.) buttermilk biscuits

In a bowl, combine all ingredients except biscuits. Cut each biscuit into four pcs. Dip each pc. halfway into honey mixture. Layer in greased 10 in. tube pan. Bake at 375 for 30-35 minutes or until golden brown. Cool 10 minutes. Invert to serving plate. Pull apart and eat.

FRUIT CRISPS   (very easy to make & good to eat)

1 box of white or yellow cake mix
1 stick of butter or margarine melted in a sm. bowl
2 cans pie filling – Your Choice (cherry, peach, blueberry, berry, apple)

Grease lightly a 13 X 9 pan. Spread pie filling on bottom of pan, spread fruit evenly. Sprinkle cake mix over top of filling, evenly. Drizzle butter or top of cake mix. Bake at 350 for 20-25 minutes or until golden brown. Cool on wire rack.

FRUIT COBBLER

1 cup bisquik mix
1 cup milk
1/2 cup butter or margarine, melted
1 cup sugar
1 can fruit, drained (Peaches, cherries, berries, apples) Don't use fruit pie filling
If using peaches, add ½ tsp. ground nutmeg

Stir together bisquick, milk, and nutmeg (optional). Pour in ungreased 8 X 8 X 2 pan. Stir in butter. Stir together sugar and fruit. Spoon over batter. Bake at 375 for 50-60 minutes or until golden brown.

KRINGLA

1 cup sugar
½ cup margarine, melted
½ tsp. salt
1 egg
1 tsp. baking powder
1 tsp. baking soda
¾ cup buttermilk
3 cups flour
1 tsp. vanilla

Mix together and chill for several hours. Roll out on lightly floured surface to about1/2 in. thickness. Cut in to thin strips. Place on ungreased cookie sheet. Make each strip into a figure 8. Bake at 450 until lightly browned. Serve with butter.

"OVER 21"
PARTY BEVERAGES

If you are parents raising teenage children, please be careful making homemade Kahlua. My intentions of making a batch, was for homemade gifts to give to my co-workers, family and friends. I calculated how much I would need which ended up being more than a few gallons. As I have stated in my recipe that it needs to sit for 3 weeks out of the sunlight. I decided to store it in the garage high on a shelf until it was time to bottle it up for gifts. Mind you, I had a couple of bottles of 190 proof Ever Clear left over that I stored for a later use. Well, leave it to two teenage boys to get curious and find it. I did not find out right away but my oldest son snuck some out in a soda bottle and took it to school and my youngest son drank enough to make him ill for a few days. Luckily they were not caught by school officials, law enforcement or me. Mostly me. After them becoming adults, they decided to share this story with their dear old mom. (Homemade Kahlua)

THIS GUIDELINE IS FOR CHOOSING THE RIGHT WINE FOR YOUR FOODS

White-Zinfandel : Spicy cuisine

Chenin Blanc: Fish and Chicken dishes

Johannisberg Riesling: Spicy ethnic foods

Sauvignon Blanc: Vegetarian dished, light appetizers and shellfish

Chardonnay: Salmon, shellfish, pastas with cream sauces and other seafood

Chardonnay Sur Lies: Salads, side dishes, veal, poultry, ham & seafood

Zinfandel: Spicy meat and poultry dishes, stews and grilled foods

Zinfandel Blanc De Noir: Cherry, lemon & raspberry flavors. Spicy & grilled foods

Cabernet Sauvignon: Beef, lamb, pastas with meat sauces and hamburgers

Cabernet Sauvignon Blanc De Noir: Desserts, quiche, sausages & sandwiches

Cardinal's Crest: Lamb, white meats & fish

STORING & SERVING WINES

Store wine out of direct sunlight

When storing for long periods of time, place bottle on its side in a cool place

Serve wines between 44-53 degrees. Serve Champagnes between 39-44 degrees

COMMON PARTY DRINKS

Old Fashioned:
2 oz. whiskey
2 lumps of sugar
2 dashes of bitters
Mix until sugar dissolves in high ball glass, Add ice.

Dry Martini:
1-2/3 oz. dry gin
1/3 oz. vermouth
Stir with ice, strain into cocktail glass. Serve with a green olive.

Bloody Mary:
1-1/2 oz. vodka
3 oz. tomato juice
½ oz. lemon juice
1 dash Worcestershire
Salt & pepper to taste
Shake well with ice. Strain into highball glass. Use celery stick for stirring.

Whiskey Sour:
2 oz. whiskey
½ tsp. sugar
Juice of ½ lemon
Shake well with ice. Strain into glass. Fill with carbonated water. Decorate with a cherry and lemon slice.

Vodka & Tonic:
2 oz. vodka
Quinine tonic
Fill 12 oz. glass with ice. Pour in vodka and fill with tonic.

Manhattan:
¾ oz. sweet vermouth
1-1/2 oz. whiskey
1 dash of bitters
Stir well with cracked ice. Strain into 3 oz. cocktail glass. Serve with a cherry

Honolulu Cooler:
1-1/2 oz. vodka
Juice of ½ lime
1 tsp. sugar
Dash of bitters & pineapple juice
Pour vodka & lime juice in tall glass, Add bitters & sugar & ice. Fill with pineapple juice. Stir well.

COMFORT EGGNOG

6 eggs
¾ cup sugar
2 cup whipped cream
1 cup cream
1 cup milk
2 cups Southern Comfort
Dash of nutmeg

Chill liquid ingredients before mixing. Separate egg whites from yolks. Beat yolks. Continue beating and add sugar. Stir in whipped cream, milk, cream and Southern Comfort. Beat egg whites and fold in. Dust with nutmeg.

ORANGE BEER

1 pint glass or jar
12 oz. cold beer
Orange juice

Pour beer into 1 pint jar or glass. Top with orange juice.

PUNCH with a PUNCH

1 pint vodka
1 liter Sprite
1 liter Hawaiian Punch
1 large punch bowl
Bag of crushed ice

Pour all ingredients in punch bowl and mix. Serve

HOMEMADE KAHLUA

2 oz. instant coffee (not freeze dried)
2-1/2 cup boiling water
Dissolve and cool

5 cups water
7 cups sugar
Boil to full rolling boil. Set aside and cool.

Mix together coffee and sugar mixtures.

1/3 cup vanilla extract
1 quart vodka or 1 quart (190 pro of Ever clear)
Add to coffee/sugar mixture.

Seal in bottles. Sit for 3 weeks.

KAHLUA RECIPES:

Kahlua & Iced Coffee
1-1/2 oz. kahlua
Chilled coffee
Cream or milk if desired
Fill tall glass with ice. Pour kahlua & chilled coffee in glass. Add milk if desired.

Kahlua & Cream
1-1/2 oz kahlua
4 oz. cream or milk
Pour kahlua over ice in glass. Add cream or milk.

Kahlua Colorado Bulldog
Kahlua & Cream recipe. Add a splash of cola. Stir briefly.

Kahlua White Russian
1 oz. Kahlua
1 oz. vodka
2 oz. cream or milk
Pour Kahlua & vodka over ice. Top with cream or milk.

Kahlua Irish & Cream
1 oz. kahlua
½ oz. Irish Cream
1 oz. cream or milk
Pour kahlua and Irish cream in a small glass. Top with cream or milk.

CANNING

Throughout this cookbook, I have mentioned that both my sons have evolved into very good cooks. Also mentioned are some of my cooking flaws. Once again, I have to admit after years of canning I had to call on my oldest son for advice. Attempting to can 100 plus jars of home grown pickles, the seals were crimping and not sealing. After explaining my situation to him, he chuckled and said "Mom, you are not filling the jars up high enough." His solution was correct . We enjoyed pickles all year long. (Helpful Hints)

HELPFUL HINTS FOR CANNING WITH THE BOILING-WATER BATH:

A boiling-water bath is a simple process of canning. Having a large garden every year I enjoy preserving my harvest to eat later in the year. It is simpler than pressure canning and a good way to preserve high acid foods, such as tomatoes. Tomatoes, cucumbers, squash/zucchini, onions and a variety of peppers are usually plentiful in my garden. We really enjoy these canned foods come winter and I always appreciate having them on hand. I rarely have to purchase stewed tomatoes which I use a lot in my soups and stews. My husband and I both enjoy munching on the pickle products.

A boiling-water bath canner is any pot deep enough to permit water to cover the jars by 1 inch, with an extra space under the jars. Do not use an aluminum pot. The canner needs a lid and rack to hold the jars. Prepare the canner by filling it halfway with water and heating the water to a boil.

Note: Yard Sales and Flea Markets are a good place to find a canner and jars.

Always examine the jars for nicks and cracks. Wash the jars in hot, soapy water. Fill the jars, leaving ¼ inch of headspace. Carefully remove air bubbles by running a nonmetallic utensil into the packed jar, releasing the air bubbles. After filling, wipe the rims and threads with a clean damp cloth. Place the lids on and screw on the metal bands.

Add or remove water in the canner as needed to provide 1-2 inches of water over the jars. Begin timing when the water returns to a boil around the jars.

Remove the jars after the processing time is complete with tongs or a canning jar lifter (The lifter is a much safer way to remove the jars). Let stand for 12-24 hours at room temperature to allow to seal properly. If the lid pops back up after pressing on it, it has not sealed. Put any unsealed jars of food in the refrigerator and use them as soon as possible. If your lids have sealed you may remove the bands (I keep them on) and store in a cool, dark, dry place. Do not let freeze.

Altitude Chart: (for processing time)

0-1,000 ft.	Time Specified
1,001 – 3,000 ft.	Add 5 minutes
3,001 – 6,000 ft.	Add 10 minutes
6,001 – 8,000 ft.	Add 15 minutes
8,001 – 10,000 ft.	Add 20 minutes

FREEZING: Boiling-water bath method is not advised for green beans or sweet corn. I blanch and freeze them in tightly wrapped (squeeze air out) freezer storage bags. I also freeze my summer squash, whole bell peppers and hot peppers.

Helpful Hints: Boil tomatoes for 5 minutes. Drain and cool. Peels slide off easily.

SWEET PICKLES

4 pounds cucumbers (3-4 in. long)
1 quart white vinegar
1 tbs. mustard seed
3 tbs. salt
¼ cup sugar

Wash cucumbers and slice ¼ in. thick. Do not peel. Put in lg. cooking pot. Mix above ingredients and pour over cucumbers. Bring to boil and simmer on low for 10 minutes. Do not overcook. Drain and discard liquid. Place cucumbers in prepared pint jars.

3 1/3 cups vinegar (5%)
5 ¾ cups sugar
2-1/4 tsp. celery seed
1 tbs. whole allspice (tie in spice bag)

Bring ingredients to a boil, stirring until sugar dissolves. Simmer on low for 5-10 minutes. Remove allspice bag. Pour hot vinegar solution over cucumbers, leaving ¼ in. headspace. Clean rims. Seal with lids and bands. Process for 10 minutes. Cool and Store.

ZUCCHINI RELISH (Sweet)

10 cups shredded zucchini (do not peel)
4 med. onions chopped
¼ cup pickling salt
5 cups sugar
2-1/4 cups white vinegar (5%)
1 tbs. celery seed
1 tbs. black pepper
1 tbs. ground turmeric

Combine zucchini, onion and salt. Cover and refrigerate for 8 hours or overnight. Rinse zucchini. Squeeze dry. Place zucchini mixture, sugar, vinegar, and spices in a lg. cooking pot. Simmer 30 minutes, stirring often. Ladle hot relish into prepared pint jars. Leave ¼ in. headspace. Clean rims. Seal with lids and bands. Process for 15 minutes. Cool and Store.

SWEET CUCUMBER RELISH (Awesome)

4 cups cucumbers grinded (do not peel)
1 cup bell pepper grinded
3 cups onion grinded
3 cups celery, chopped very fine
1 – 4 oz. jar of red pimento peppers, drained and chopped
¾ cup salt
4 cups cold water
7 cups sugar
1 tbs. mustard seed (heaping)
1 tbs. celery seed
4 cups white vinegar

Make brine first. Mix salt and water. Mix well. Add all vegetables except pimento peppers. Sit 8 hours or overnight in refrigerator. I use a food processor to chop the vegetables. Do not puree them. Drain (do not rinse) and squeeze out salt water. In lg. cooking pot add sugar, mustard seed, celery seed and vinegar. Bring to boil, stirring until sugar dissolves. Add vegetables and pimentos. Simmer for 10 minutes, stirring often. Ladle into ½ pint or jelly jars, leaving ¼ in. headspace. Clean rim and seal with lids and bands. Process in water bath for 15 minutes. Cool and store.

PICKLED BEETS

7 lbs. 2 to 2-1/2 inch diameter beets
4 cups vinegar (5%)
1-1/2 tsp canning salt
2 cups sugar
2 cups water
2 cinnamon sticks
12 whole cloves
1 tbs. whole allspice

Wash beets. Trim off tops leaving 1 in. of stem. Boil lg. pot of water. Add beets. Cook until tender. Test by poking with a slender sharp knife. If knife slides out easily the beets are ready. Drain off water. Place beets in sink and cool. Trim off tops and roots. Peel should easily slide off. Slice beets into ¼ in. slices into prepared pint jars. Put cinnamon, cloves and allspice in a tied cheesecloth bag. Boil vinegar, salt, sugar, water and spice bag. Simmer 5-10 minutes. Remove spice bag. Fill jars with sliced beets with hot vinegar solution., leaving ¼ in. headspace. Clean rims and seal with lids and bands. Process in water bath for 15 minutes. Cool and store.

GARLIC DILL PICKLES

4 pounds cucumbers (3-4 in.)
6 cups water
4-1/2 cups cider vinegar (5%)
6 tbs. pickling salt
¾ tsp. crushed red pepper
16 sm. cloves of garlic, split in half
16 heads of fresh dill

Wash cucumbers and remove 1/16 inch of blossom end. In a 3 qt. saucepan, combine, water, vinegar, salt and crushed pepper. Bring to a boil, simmer 5 minutes. Place 2 pcs. garlic and 1 head of dill in bottom of prepared pint jars. Firmly pack cucumbers in each jar. Place 2 more pcs. of garlic and 1 head of dill on top of cucumbers. Pour hot vinegar mixture over cucumbers, leaving ½ in. headspace. Remove trapped air. Wipe rims clean. Seal with lids and bands. Process for 10 minutes. Cool and store.

SALSA

7-8 cups peeled, chopped tomatoes

Note: Place tomatoes in boiling water for 5 minutes. Remove, drain and cool. Skins should slide off easily. I like to chop the tomatoes briefly in a food processor. Do not puree.

2 cups Peppers (remove seeds)

Note: If you like your salsa hot, use hot peppers of your choice. WARNING: When handling hot peppers, wear thin latex gloves and do not rub your eyes. (or your hands & eyes will burn all night) If you like your salsa medium, use ½ hot peppers and ½ bell peppers. If you like your salsa mild, use all bell peppers or sweet peppers.

3 cups chopped onion
1 cup sugar
2 cups vinegar
1 tsp. salt
1 tsp. cilantro (optional)

In a lg. cooking pot simmer all ingredients together for 5-10 minutes. Do not drain but when ladling into prepared pint jars let some of the liquid drain off. Clean rims. Seal with lids and bands. Process for 15 minutes. Cool and Store.

SPAGHETTI SAUCE

5 cups chopped bell pepper
10 cups chopped onion
½ cup minced garlic
1 cup oil
11-1/2 pounds tomatoes, peeled and chopped
4 – cans tomato paste (12 oz. each)
1 cup sugar
¼ cup salt
2 tbs. dried oregano
2 tsp. dried basil
1 tbs. lemon juice

Cook peppers, onion and garlic in oil in a 12 qt. cooking pot. Cook over medium heat, stirring constantly until tender. Add tomatoes, paste, sugar, salt, oregano and basil. Bring to boil. Reduce heat and simmer for 30 minutes or until thickened. Stirring often. Remove from heat and add lemon juice. Pour into prepared pint jars leaving ½ of headspace. Remove air bubbles. Clean rims. Seal with lids and bands. Process for 30 minutes. Cool and store.

STEWED TOMATOES

12 cups tomatoes, peeled, and chopped
3 cups chopped onion
2 cups chopped bell pepper
1 tsp. salt (optional)

Mix all together in cooking pot. Simmer for 10 minutes. Ladle into prepared jars. Note: If you just want tomatoes only. Don't add onion and peppers. I like them like this so they are ready to put in my soups, chili and stews.
Leave ½ in. headspace. Clean rims. Seal with lids and bands. Process in pints for 20 minutes. Cool and Store.

TOMATO SAUCE

20 pounds ripe tomatoes, peeled and chopped
2 onions minced
2-3 bell peppers chopped
6 stalks of celery chopped
2-3 carrots chopped

Puree all ingredients in a blender or food processor. Simmer for 1 hour, stirring often. Pour into prepared jelly or pint jars. Clean rim. Seal with lids and bands. Process for 30 minutes. Cool and Store.

JAMS & JELLIES

Ripe fruit
Sugar
Pectin

I make jams and jellies every year. I have found the best recipe for these come from the inside of the pectin box. Follow the measurements accurately, using ripe fruits and you will have delicious preserves to enjoy all year.

Take advantage of your friends and families fruit trees. Pick and preserve when the fruits are ripe. Buy fruits that are in season. I enjoy picking wild berries. Take the family along. Its not only good exercise but it will bring memories around the breakfast table when enjoying your freshly made jams and jellies.

Index

Cabbage Rolls 67
Corn Beef Hash 71
Cranberry Meatballs 73
Crock Pot Stew 64
Hamburger Casserole 74
Hamburger Delight 74
Hearty Meatballs 72
Home Made Salami 75
Manicotti 68
Marinated Steak 72
Meat Loaf 68
Minute Steaks 76
Pepper Steak 70
Pot of Chili 65
Prime Rib 66
Stroganoff 75
Stuffed Peppers 67
Sweet & Sour Beef 70
Sweet & Sour Meatballs 73
Taco Casserole 67
Tacos 65

CHICKEN

Almond Chicken 82
Breaded Chicken Breasts 78
Cashew Chicken 87
Chicken A La King 83
Chicken Cacciatore 81
Chicken Cordon Bleu 85
Chicken & Dumplings 79
Chicken Enchiladas 85
Chicken Fajitas 84
Chicken Kabobs 83
Chicken Pot Pie 80
Chicken Strips 88
Chicken Wontons 88
Five Spice Chicken Stir Fry 87
Hawaiian Chicken 81
Lemon-Garlic Chicken 82
Make Ahead Turkey 89
Parmesan Chicken 78
Quesadilla 84
Spicy Chicken Stir Fry 86
Sweet & Sour Chicken Stir Fry 86

PORK

Calgary Ribs 93
Chinese Ribs 93
Chops with Spicy Peanut Sauce 97
Fried Pork Chops 96
Frisco Chops 96
Grilled Chops 97
Grilled Honey Garlic Chops 97

Hawaiian Ribs 92
Mandarin Medallions 95
Medallions in a Brandy-Pear Sauce 95
Mushroom Medallions 94
Orange Style Ribs 93
Oven Baked BBQ Chops 96
Pizza 100
Polish Casserole 98
Pork Egg Rolls 100
Pork Fajitas 99
Pork Kabobs 99
Pork Medallions 94
Pork Stir Fry 98
Sausage Stromboli 101
Smoked Beans 101
Smoked Boston Butt 99
Smokey Ribs 92
Tangy Ribs 92

FISH-SEAFOOD

BBQ Trout 106
Blackened Cat Fish 105
Crab Primavera 104
Fried Cat Fish 105
Shrimp'ly Delicious 104
Springtime Crappie 106
Tuna Casserole 107

POTATOES & VEGETABLE SIDE DISH

Calico Beans 115
Cashew Asparagus 117
Cauliflower 118
Corn 120
Creamy Broccoli Casserole 118
Deep Fried Okra & Mushrooms 115
Dill Potatoes Au Gratin 114
Double Stuffed Potatoes 110
Easy Baked Potatoes 110
Eggplant 121
Good Ole Fried Tators 112
Green Beans 118
Hashbrown Casserole 112
Kool Peppers 119
Parsley Potatoes 111
Pork Fried Rice 116
Potato Patties 113
Scalloped Potatoes 111
Spanish Rice 116
Spinach Manicotti 117
Steak Fries 113
Stuffing 113
Supreme Potatoes 111

BREADS - ROLLS - BISCUITS - MUFFINS

CAKES & FROSTINGS

CAKES

FROSTING

PIES

COOKIES - CANDY - TREATS

"OVER 21" PARTY BEVERAGES

CANNING RECIPES